New Normal

"Beneath the weight of ongoing conflicts and natural disasters, political upheaval, and social unrest, we need to be anchored by words that express our praise, fears, laments, and questions to the God we love and serve. These thoughtful prayers compiled by Dr. Paul Mercer are a profound gift for personal and corporate worship in these challenging days."

—TIM COSTELLO,
executive director, Micah Australia

"Paul Mercer offers us Spirit-fueled congregational liturgies for a new generation. Following the liturgical calendar and drawing on a breadth of Christian theology, these liturgies are steeped in the Christian tradition. And with poetic creativity, they shape the church to reflect the tenderness of Jesus today. I highly recommend *New Normal* to pastors and worship leaders."

—MARK GLANVILLE,
associate professor of pastoral theology, and Old Testament scholar,
Regent College, Vancouver, British Columbia

"During the isolating time of Covid-19, Dr. Paul Mercer took the initiative with our Bayside Uniting Church congregation to engage us in prayers of openness before God, togetherness with one another, and responsiveness to the Scriptures. These prayers have become a catalyst in helping people encounter God through meaningful articulation, creative embodiment, and honest expressiveness amidst truly trying times."

—CRAIG BLACKBURN,
pastor, Bayside Uniting Church, Queensland, Australia

"Dr. Paul Mercer's inspirational prayers open avenues to people in all walks of life to approach God amidst various types of distress—grief, loss, illness, homelessness, domestic violence, and mental health challenges. This book provides a pathway where people can seek God's peace, protection, and love through times of lament as well as praise. It will also be a resource for those who are supporting others going through the stresses and crises of different seasons of life."

—BRONWYN HERBERT,
social worker, Brisbane, Australia

"Paul's beautiful and poetic communal prayers sew together threads of Scripture with the day-to-day challenges and joys of our lives, drawing on Old Testament patterns of worship that anchor us in our earthly existence through seasons of weather as well as liturgy. His eyes range over the personal as well as the global, reminding the short-sighted of the wider world and the long-sighted that there are next-door neighbors. The pattern of corporate poetic liturgy in these prayers will encourage church leaders and congregations to think hard about how we draw near to God together and will be a blessing to all who incorporate them into their congregational worship."

—GREG ANDERSON,
bishop, Northern Territory for the Anglican Church, Australia

"Paul Mercer is known by many as a physician of the body. His heart for people was shown to me as he cared for my parents in the closing years of their lives, where he demonstrated an understanding of the interaction between body, mind, and spirit. His personal faith has inspired this book of liturgical prayers, which are balm to our soul as they remind us of God's goodness, promises, and truth."

—DAVID AND HELEN SMALLBONE,
managers and promoters, Christian music industry

New Normal

Discerning the Rhythm of Lament, Thanks, and Praise in Bad Times and Good

PAUL MERCER

Foreword by Beth M. Stovell

RESOURCE *Publications* · Eugene, Oregon

NEW NORMAL
Discerning the Rhythm of Lament, Thanks, and Praise in Bad Times and Good

Copyright © 2024 Paul Mercer. All rights reserved. Except for brief quotations in critical publications or reviews, no part of this book may be reproduced in any manner without prior written permission from the publisher. Write: Permissions, Wipf and Stock Publishers, 199 W. 8th Ave., Suite 3, Eugene, OR 97401.

Resource Publications
An Imprint of Wipf and Stock Publishers
199 W. 8th Ave., Suite 3
Eugene, OR 97401

www.wipfandstock.com

PAPERBACK ISBN: 979-8-3852-1554-6
HARDCOVER ISBN: 979-8-3852-1555-3
EBOOK ISBN: 979-8-3852-1556-0
VERSION NUMBER 12/09/24

All Scripture quotations, unless otherwise indicated, are taken from the *COMMON ENGLISH BIBLE*. © Copyright 2011 *COMMON ENGLISH BIBLE*. All rights reserved. Used by permission (www.CommonEnglishBible.com).

Scripture quotations marked NRSV are taken from New Revised Standard Version Bible, copyright © 1989 National Council of the Churches of Christ in the United States of America. Used by permission. All rights reserved worldwide.

Cover photo by Jonathan Dass Photography (2024). Used by permission.

Cover painting by Helen Monoghan (2003). Used by permission.

This book is dedicated to my patient, Helen, whose life is nearing its end from a rare adenocarcinoma of the duodenum.

In 2014, Helen was involved in a serious motor vehicle accident and suffered a head injury, which impacted her short-term memory and caused her to have left-sided weakness. She now lives in a care facility for the aged.

For the long periods of isolation during the pandemic, she was sustained by God's love. "God sat me on his lap," she describes, "and I knew I was loved. He told me black was a 'good color.'"

In 2003, many years before Helen's accident, she painted a picture of God caring for his world, which she called, "The Father's Love." The inspiration for this painting came from Psalm 139:13: "you are the one who created my innermost parts, you knit me together while I was still in my mother's womb." In 2004, "The Father's Love" won a category award at the Blake Prize for Religious Art in Australia.

This painting continues to hang over Helen's bed. Though the motor vehicle accident impaired her artistic abilities, she continues to love to color and draw as time goes by.

I visited Helen early in the COVID lockdown, dressed in full PPE, after she had developed a painful case of shingles. This ailment seemed to be an apt metaphor for the painful pressures that we were all facing during that time, and I was struck by how bravely she faced this new setback.

I continue to be inspired and surprised by Helen's perseverance and enduring smile as she walks the long road of suffering, comforted by God's abiding love for her and for everyone around her.

Contents

Foreword by Beth M. Stovell | *ix*

Preface | *xiii*

Acknowledgements | *xv*

Introduction | *xvii*

Prayers for the Season of Advent | 1

Prayers for the Season of Christmastide | 23

Prayers for the Season after Epiphany | 33

Prayers for the Season of Lent | 59

Prayers for the Season of Easter | 105

Prayers for the Season of Ordinary Time | 137

Postface | 249

Bibliography | *255*

Foreword

Praying with the Long Line of Voices

There is power when we pray together. Raising our voices together before the God of all creation, we stand in the long line of voices before us that date all the way back to the people in the Bible themselves. When we speak the words of the Bible and those words are shaped to meet our lives today, we are offered an opportunity to draw the past into the present and see a vision for the future. This is one of the great gifts of Paul Mercer's liturgical prayers. Paul offers us words to respond to the beautiful complexity of our lives before the multifaceted greatness of God.

I had the joy of teaching Paul during my Reading and Preaching Biblical Poetry course at Regent College in 2022.[1] The class was full of excellent students, who had meaningful conversations about the value of biblical poetry and how its form as well as its content spoke truth and healing into people's lives in the ancient times and can continue to do so today. I was struck at the time by Paul's excitement for the course and his unique insights as a doctor and as a writer. He began the process of writing these prayers just prior to the course. I was honored to be among the first readers of what would become this book.

Paul's excitement for God's word is evident in every prayer in this book. His unique perspective as a doctor offers awareness of the deep pain, grief, and loss in our congregations today, and this awareness helps shape his insightful and transformative prayers. Yet his book is also filled with the joy, awe, and wonder of celebrating God.

---

1. While I am typically a Professor of Old Testament at Ambrose Seminary of Ambrose University in Calgary, I sometimes teach for Regent College, where I completed my Master of Christian Studies degree.

Foreword

In this book, Paul offers paths with the Psalms that are consistent with what Old Testament scholars have explored. In *From Whom No Secrets are Hid*, Walter Brueggemann explains why the Psalms meet us in every season of our souls and address every kind of emotion.[2] The Psalms were a key part of the ancient Israelites' worship, reflecting the needs of the entire community and the individuals within it. The Psalms retold the stories of their ancestors and their relationship with God and reminded the people of the covenant God had made with them. At the same time, the people worshiped God through their prayers while also exploring the complex emotions that come from living in a complicated world.

In the foreword to Brueggemann's book, Brent Strawn adds that the Psalms offer a way for us to disclose our secrets before God.[3] Through the Psalms, we can speak about our deepest pain, fears, grief, and find words for them. Through this secret-sharing, we can be freed for God to heal those spaces.

In *Journey through the Psalms*, Denise Dombkowski Hopkins explains that sometimes this expression of struggle through the Psalms may be the only avenue we have for these difficult emotions, and we not only express this individually but in communities.[4] In times when we feel hopeful, the person beside us might be struggling. In times when we are hurting, the person beside us can offer encouragement to us by speaking the Psalms. As Dombkowski Hopkins explains, "by allowing someone to express negative feelings instead of making the person feel ashamed to express them, we hear that person into speech; we empower her or him. We help to keep open the disoriented one's relationship with God through the only avenue of communication open to the person at the moment."[5] We also can rejoice with another when they are rejoicing. When we speak the Psalms in their vast diversity, we give room for these emotions of others. We can "rejoice with those who rejoice and weep with those who weep," to echo the Apostle Paul (Rom 12:15).

In the extraordinary collection of prayers in *New Normal*, Paul Mercer offers us many gifts. First, he creates a path with the Psalms that reminds us of God's great story with his people as well as a way to get involved. Second, he gives us a way to disclose the secret, difficult feelings within us through

---

2. Brueggemann, *From Whom No Secrets are Hid*.
3. Strawn, "The Psalms and the Practices of Disclosure," xiii–xxiv.
4. Hopkins, *Journey through the Psalms*.
5. Hopkins, *Journey through the Psalms*, 114.

Foreword

the prayers of the Psalms. Third, he charts a way for us to rejoice together and also weep together. Fourth, he makes space for us to walk beside one another as we grow through the spirituality of the Psalms, not only as individuals, but also as a community.

All of this leads towards the personal and communal healing, restoration, reconciliation, and joy that we all need.

Beth M. Stovell
Calgary, Alberta
August 2024

Preface

This book would not have found its place and voice without the COVID-19 pandemic. Though tragic, the liminal space that opened during the time of lockdown created an opening for the imagination, where the Spirit could prompt constructive expressions of praise.

These prayers of lament, thanksgiving, and praise arose out of worship at Bayside Uniting Church after May 2020, when the Covid pandemic challenged worship "as usual," since services were restricted to online gatherings.

During this time, I felt stirred to discern how I could contribute positively within our faith community. Over Easter 2020, I prepared a YouTube presentation entitled, "Coming, Ready or Not," after which I recognized the possibility of writing congregational prayers, both for in-person gatherings as well as online use.[6]

These prayers were based on the weekly morning and evening liturgical readings of each Sunday as the pandemic gripped the world stage. What emerged was an eclectic set of integrated Old and New Testament "psalms" that follow the liturgical year. As we gather in Christ, amidst both "bad times" and "good times," we can receive the strange gift of a "new normal" world. May the circulation of these "new normal" prayers be to the glory of God.

Paul Mercer
Manly West, Australia
September 2024

---

6. See https://www.youtube.com/watch?v=eGFJE3srdW4.

Acknowledgements

I am very grateful to the leadership team at Bayside Uniting Church in Manly West, Queensland (Australia), who ran with the suggestion of preparing online congregational prayers alongside the liturgical rhythm of Scripture readings amidst the context of COVID lockdowns and the resulting shift to online worship. As with many other worshipping communities, we settled into a hybrid online / offline format. Many fellow worshippers at Bayside Uniting have encouraged me and provided valuable feedback on these prayers. I thank, especially, Craig Blackburn, our current minister, and Ian Lord, a past minister, for their support. My friends Steve Bradbury and Dave Andrews also provided helpful feedback.

Early on in the pandemic, I joined in evening prayer times with Health Serve Australia (an INGO that I Chair) after our executive officer called key supporters into a nightly prayer time. Soon after, a related organization, the Christian Medical and Dental Fellowship of Australia, began weekly prayer together online. These two prayer groups, in association with my local church, have reinforced the encouragement of praying together as Christians and have helped me to sand off some rough edges and maintain the humility I needed for this project.

For over a decade, I have been involved in a theological reading group with Charles Ringma, a professor emeritus of Regent College in Vancouver, British Columbia. Just prior to the pandemic, Charles acted as a "doula" by encouraging me to join his Holy Scribbler writing community (www.holyscribblers.blogspot.com). Their constructive feedback has kept me on task, and through our Scribbler writing retreats, I encountered the Celtic spirituality of the Northumbria community. Charles has been a patient, encouraging mentor.

During Covid, our reading group read Michael Gorman's *Participating in Christ,* which I found to be very helpful and challenging. Because I

Acknowledgements

was reading Gorman's book while writing these prayers, there are echoes of his writing in some of the prayers.

In July 2022, I enrolled in a Regent College online summer school course with Beth Stovell on the subject of biblical poetry. In this accelerated learning context, *New Normal* moved toward its completion. I am grateful to Beth and fellow learners in this course.

Then in June 2024, I attended a Regent Summer School on Paul's spirituality, which was led by Michael Gorman. This course encouraged me to think further about prayer in the cannon of Scripture.

My editor, Karen Hollenbeck Wuest, has further inspired and shaped the book. She orientated me to finish writing for a yearly liturgical pattern, and the book's work has benefited immensely from this focus.

I would also like to acknowledge Keira Reid, who has been a wonderful support in typing and arranging this material.

The many hours of reading canonical Scripture passages and creating this poetry of praise has only been possible through the support of my family, especially my wife, Katrina, my mother-in-law, Bronwyn, and my father, John. Katrina has graciously given me the space and time I needed to finish this book and has offered feedback and encouragement at just the right time.

Introduction

In *The Cost of Discipleship*, Dietrich Bonhoeffer pointedly observes that Christ "stands between us" and our neighbors.[1] Because Christ "stands between us," Bonhoeffer offers two pertinent observations. First, intercession is the most promising way to reach our neighbors. Second, corporate prayer offered in the name of Christ is the "purest form of fellowship."[2]

The COVID-19 pandemic declared by both the United Nations and the World Health Organization on 3 March 2020 created many challenges for both the people of God and the world in which we live. For a time, social distancing was unexpectedly mandated for us all. Lockdowns closed our churches, and many people became online refugees. In the context of COVID-19, everyone was a potential carrier, and many succumbed to this illness.

In the strange, "new normal" of lockdown, I began to ache with the loss of corporate spiritual practices and the presence of Jesus among his gathered people. As services migrated to livestream platforms, I offered to prepare regular congregational prayers based on the liturgical readings for the Sunday online services at my church. I started to write prayers of praise, lament, and thanksgiving in a monthly rhythm, drawing on both Old and New Testament Scriptures. As these "new creation" psalms began to flow, I found myself writing more consistently within the cyclical rhythm of the liturgical year.

Apart from COVID-19, many other cross-cutting cultural challenges influenced this prayer mix: Black lives matter, domestic violence, loneliness, calls back to freedom, the Russian invasion of Ukraine, climate

---

1. Bonhoeffer, *Cost of Discipleship*, 88.
2. Bonhoeffer, 88.

Introduction

change, along with other pressing concerns, including the grief of losing loved ones from this new pandemic illness.

Both the stain of sin and the flowing river of God's love crisscross the pages of Scripture. In writing these prayers, I have entered into a conversation with biblical poetry and metaphor, joining the cries of lament in Scripture with the ache of our present times. I have also discovered the power of praise in reflecting the overwhelming hope of the gospel of Jesus Christ.

Some of these prayers highlight particular voices, some add rhythm, and many hold dialectic tension between a passage from Scripture as it encounters our times. While I have tried to be a "church mouse" in this adventure, I confess that at times my own voice creeps into prayer lines. As a medical doctor, I have a heart for healing, and these prayers offer praise to God, who loves the whole world—all of our neighbors—and desires for us to be in fellowship through the Holy Spirit, which can bring us healing and hope in both bad times and good.

A significant body of Scripture is written in poetic form, including stand-alone poems, psalms, and much of the prophetic writings. Biblical poetry often arises from a heartfelt cry and seeks to offer praise to our loving Creator God. Some biblical poetry captures the tension between God's judgement and love or the human experience of darkness against light, and some adapts secular praise in order to bring glory to God.

The poetry of praise often reflects a posture of both wrestling and patient waiting on God within the act of worship. A poem may start with a particular poet's praise and become the praise of the people of God. This dynamic of moving from the personal to the corporate captured my imagination and inspired me to write praise for our particular time in history.

The poetic wrestling in Scripture identifies many pressures, fears, and threats that any generation may face. I am not normally a poet, but the circumstances of the pandemic have informed my journey of following Jesus and prompted me to seek a liturgical expression of prayer for today. My hope is that these prayers gleaned from Scripture will bless others in my generation as well as those in future generations.

It has been helpful for me to understand these prayers as intercession for our neighbors and as a way of seeking to share the "purest" fellowship, as Bonhoeffer describes it, by participating in corporate prayer.

I accept full responsibility for any unhelpful and misleading arrangement of Scripture in these prayers, which have been written at times through extended contemplation of rich wells in Scripture's voice and at

INTRODUCTION

others under the pressure of deadlines, a heavy work schedule, and unexpected demands.

I wrote these prayers over a period of four years, and as the liturgical year began to fill in, I occasionally chose some retrospective reading dates to fill the gaps. Thus the readings for each Sunday do not always line up with the particular liturgical year (or sometimes the season) in which they were written. All in all, I have written these prayers as a composite of the liturgical year, and so I have occasionally strayed from the established rhythm of the cannon's narrative, which follows a three-year cycle.

To all who access these new psalms of praise, may our whole being find its center in the resounding praise of God, whom together we know as Father, Son, and Spirit.

Prayers for the Season of Advent

ADVENT: WEEK 1A

In Praise of God, our Teacher

Jeremiah 33:14–16; Psalm 25:1–10;
1 Thessalonians 3:9–13; Luke 21:25–36

Leader:	We give our praise to God, who is good and who does the right thing.
	With compassion, God teaches sinners which way to go.
All:	Lord, teach us your truth. Lead us along the path of faithful love, which never ever ends. Do not let anyone who hopes in you be put to shame.
Men:	We are a people who have done many dumb things. Please do not remember the sins of our youth. Teach us what it takes to be just and do right.
Women:	Lord, for the sake of your good name, forgive our sins, which are many. Teach us through the way of the cross to stand in Christ alone.
Leader:	We give our praise to Christ our Savior. Teach us to grow in love for each other and to see everyone as created in God's image. May we be prepared when you come as the master of your people.
All:	Wisdom alone comes from you. Teach us so that your ways are the center of our curriculum. We long for your coming in the clouds. We want to be ready when your redemption comes near.
Men:	Lord, we are willing learners, and we offer our lives to you. We confess that your time is coming soon. Prepare

	us, shape us, and strengthen our hearts for kingdom service.
Women:	Don't let us down, Lord. Remember your faithful love. We want to keep our eyes on your kingdom coming. In the place of drinking parties, teach us the rhythms of the Spirit. When we are filled with anxiety, teach us to stay the course and to be mindful of your faithfulness in any crisis, any pandemic.
Leader:	When the cosmos is in turmoil, the winds roar, and the seas surge, teach us how to sing in the storm. When the world is in disarray, teach us how to pray for your centering presence in our lives and to stand in the liberating power of the gospel.
All:	As the ever-learning people of God, we honor the gift of your teaching in our lives. You are preparing us to be blameless in holiness.

ADVENT: WEEK 1B

Expectation

Malachi 3:1–4; Luke 1:68–79; Philippians 1:3–10

All: Praise the Lord! We gather in the awareness that Jesus, our Lord, has promised to be with us always. We pray together with a sense of joy that by the power of the Spirit, Jesus meets with us today. We are his body.

Women: Look! The Lord you are seeking will come to his temple, to the world he has created.

Men: Look! The messenger of the covenant is coming. The incarnate Son of the Lord of heaven is with us.

Women: Look! God has spoken through the mouth of the prophets of Israel. He is coming with deep compassion, bringing the light of Christ to all who are sitting in darkness.

Men: Look! The path is cleared. God is moving into our neighborhoods. In his mercy, he is bringing salvation to his enemies. To all who are walking in the shadows of death, a newborn King issues an invitation to follow him onto the paths of peace.

Women: Look! The mercy of God is coming in the arrival of the advent child. The dawn of heaven is breaking into our sinful lives.

Men: Look! We have been shown the way of repentance, the way revealed to Abraham. God's love always rescues. This is the way of a refiner's fire, a cleaner's soap.

All:	As the newly rescued people of the dawn of heaven, we commit to serve God without fear. As people of the light, we commit to serve in holiness and to do what is good and right in God's eyes, as long as we shall live.
Women:	Look again! The one who started a good work in us will stay until the job is done. We expect to be transformed into the image of Christ Jesus.
Men:	Look again! God keeps us in his heart, and we keep one another in our hearts. We expect to remain partners in the gospel, partners in God's grace.
Women:	Look again! We are growing in love, complemented by knowledge and insight.
Men:	Look again! Our lives are being filled with gladness, and joy is flowing into our community.
All:	Today God's redeeming, restoring salvation is with us. Our lives are the fruit of the gospel of Christ. Hallelujah, all expectation is fulfilled in Jesus Christ!

ADVENT: WEEK 2A

Prayer as a Spiritual Roadmap

Isaiah 40:1–11; Psalm 85:1–2, 8–13; 2 Peter 3:8–15a; Mark 1:1–8

All:	We raise our voice and shout, "Clear the Lord's way, make a level highway for your coming into our faithless world."
Men:	Our grateful hearts attend to the words of the father, saying, "You are my Son, whom I dearly love; in you I find happiness."[1] Your happiness is infectious. As prodigals, we long for your embrace.
Women:	Our grateful hearts give thanks that the penalty has been paid. With all humanity, we rejoice in the glory of your salvation.
Leader:	Promise-keeping God, we are waiting for a new heaven and a new earth, the place where righteousness and justice are at home.
All:	Your kindness, O Lord, leads you to forgive us. Your grace covers our sin. As we remember the cleansing of baptism, revive our hearts with the refreshing breath of your Spirit.
Men:	Your salvation is very close to those who honor you. We surrender all into the open space of your faithful love and truth.

---

1. Mark 1:11.

Prayers for the Season of Advent

Women: We hear and receive the gentle breeze of your comfort. Comfort us again. Bring us from the wilderness of panic and fear on the arm of your love.

Leader: Protect us, Holy Trinity, from returning to foolish ways. Keep us in the sweet union of righteousness and peace. Be our roadmap in days of anxiety and distress.

All: Loving one, you embrace us as Father, Son, and Spirit. We confess that you only give us what is good.

Men: In a united voice, we call on you to be kind to your world. Break the oppression of pandemic grief and loss. Comfort all who are afraid and in anguish. Give to all their daily bread. Bring shelter to the evicted and homeless.

Women: Amidst the troubles of our world, God, we call on you to speak the words of peace. Bind up the evil of sexual exploitation, racial abuse, and craven greed. May your truth spring from the ground in every place on earth.

Leader: As we live in your good, but troubled, world, strengthen us in these days of trial. Fill us with the activity of your compassion. Comfort our hearts during this wilderness time and move us toward your good future in the power of the Spirit. Amen.

ADVENT: WEEK 2B

Watching and Waiting Praise

Ruth 3:1–5; 4:13–17; Psalm 127; Hebrews 9:24–28; Mark 12:38–44

All sit.

All: Following Jesus together, we walk the journey of faith.

Men: *(Pause.)* We are silent, eagerly awaiting the love song of our God.

Women: *(Open hands.)* We are praying, eagerly awaiting the life-giving spirit.

Men: *(Raise hands.)* We are praising, eagerly awaiting your restoration in our times of distress and failure.

Women: *(Stand and rotate.)* We dance for joy. With all creation, we eagerly await our redeemer.

Leader: *(All stand.)* May the Lord be blessed! Our redeemer Christ is the Savior of the world. Whosoever will believe, come with us!

All: *(Remain standing.)* Following Jesus together, we embrace the rhythms of grace.

Women: *(All sit, pause.)* We are silent. We eagerly look to your security and the embrace of your everlasting arms.

Men: *(Open hands.)* We are praying as we face the suffering and struggle of life. We discern your sustaining mercy, drawing us to your side.

Prayers for the Season of Advent

Women: *(Raise hands.)* In eagerness, we await the words of comfort from our risen Lord, who is always willing to assure us that our sins are forgiven. Hallelujah!

Men: *(Stand and rotate.)* We are dancing with joy. We eagerly await the reappearance of Christ, who in glory will complete our salvation.

Leader: *(All stand.)* Our redeemer Christ has come into the world at Bethlehem. He took on the sins of many on a cross outside Jerusalem. As our resurrected Lord, he will come into our history again so that every knee will bow, to the glory of the father.

All: May the Lord be blessed!

Men: *(Sit.)* Watch out for all who strut their own stuff.

Women: *(Sit.)* Watch out for all who seek public acclamation and kudos.

Men: *(Stand.)* Watch out for all who want to be movers and shakers and see their name in lights.

Women: *(Stand.)* Watch out for all who cheat the vulnerable, especially orphans and widows.

Men: *(Sit.)* Watch out for all who show off their spirituality. Preserve us from their long, hollow prayers.

Women: *(Sit.)* Watch out for all who only give God their spare change, their leftover time, and limp friendship.

Leader: *(Remain sitting.)* May the Lord be blessed! Father, Son and Spirit, every good gift comes from you. You watch over us so that all may go well for us.
You watch out for us, for you are our security and peace. You watch with us and sustain us in the callings of earth keeping and reconciliation.
You will remain with us to the end of the age.

All: *(Stand.)* Jesus, our redeemer, the one we eagerly await, accept our surrender to the power of your salvation today. By grace, we give everything we are and have to you. Amen (*shout*). To the Lord (*clap clap*)! To the Lord (*clap clap*)!

ADVENT: WEEK 3A

Sweet Song of Salvation

Zephaniah 3:14-20; Isaiah 12:2-6; Philippians 4:4-7; Luke 3:7-18

Leader: Sing to the Lord because he is doing glorious things.
Proclaim Jesus everywhere.
Rejoice and exalt in your hearts.
Declare that God's name is exalted!

Chorus: Shout and sing for joy.
Our shame is changed into praise.
We are drawing with joy from the
springs of salvation.

Men: God is indeed my salvation.
I will trust God in a world of fear.
I will fear no evil because the Lord is my strength and shield.

Chorus: Shout and sing for joy.
Our shame is changed into praise.
We are drawing with joy from the
springs of salvation.

Women: Our God is gathering us in Christ.
Rejoice and be glad in the Lord always.
He creates calm with his love.
He delivers the lame.

Chorus: Shout and sing for joy.
Our shame is changed into praise.
We are drawing with joy from the
springs of salvation.

Prayers for the Season of Advent

Men: We call on the Name of Jesus,
Save us from the trials of this time.
Our trust is fully in Christ.
We affirm that we will not be anxious about anything.

Chorus: Shout and sing for joy.
Our shame is changed into praise.
We are drawing with joy from the
springs of salvation.

Women: We have been baptized with the
fire of the spirit.
The peace of God keeps
our hearts and minds safe in Christ.

Chorus: Shout and sing for joy.
Our shame is changed into praise.
We are drawing with joy from the
springs of salvation.

Men: Sweet, gracious salvation is the
DNA of God the Father, Son, and Spirit.
In this strength, we are committed
to share our food with the hungry and to deal with everyone in gentleness.

Chorus: Shout and sing for joy, for
Our shame is changed into praise.
We are drawing with joy from the
springs of salvation.

Women: Saving God, you are always near.
Remember to gather all who are outcasts.
In gladness, we will share our clothes.
In kindness, we will deal fairly and honorably with all.
All our action comes from your love.

Chorus: Shout and sing for joy.
Our shame is changed into praise.
We are drawing with joy from the
springs of salvation.

All: Our wonder, O Lord, overflows.
When we recognize your desire to sing over our lives,
we are blown away with joy.
Hallelujah for your sweet song of salvation.

Advent: Week 3 A

Leader: Bring your requests, prayers, petitions, and thanksgiving to God, our Savior.
All: *(Pray in silence.)*
Leader: And the people said,
All: Amen, Amen, Amen!

ADVENT: WEEK 3B

In the Praise Zone

Zephaniah 3:14–20; Isaiah 12:2–6; Philippians 4:4–7; Luke 3:7–18

Leader: In your presence, Lord, your people celebrate the great reversal of salvation. We praise you for removing the burdens of sin. We shout out your name on the straight path of love.

Children: Our eyes are wide open with expectation. Our young hearts are truly free because you really, really love us. Hooray!

Women: We sing your song of praise as if the siege of sin has ended—as if our adversary, the devil, has departed through the power of the cross of Christ.

Men: We cheer for the King of Salvation as our stony hearts are restored for life. We don't depend on bloodlines because the Good News of Jesus has come.

All: Jesus. (*Clap, clap, clap.*) You invite us into the praise zone. (*Clap, clap, clap.*)

Leader: A roar of praise rises as all of humanity beholds your salvation, the calming presence of cruciform love.

Children: With Jesus as King, we aren't afraid. We wave and shout your name, Jesus. (*Clap, clap, clap.*)

Women: We trust in you, not in well-intended rituals. You defend our honor through the storms of faith. You deliver the lame. You gather the outcast. You change our shame into praise.

Advent: Week 3B

Men:	In Jesus we won't worry. It's a joy to be happy. You are always close by. We pray that your peace will keep our hearts and minds safe, O Lord.
All:	Jesus. (*Clap, clap, clap.*) You invite us into the praise zone. (*Clap, clap, clap.*)
Leader:	We are not worthy to untie your shoelaces. Sift the chaff from our lives so that we will produce the goods of grace.
Children:	Help us share our food and toys.
Women:	Keep us on track with love.
Men:	Keep our hearts content with your bread each day.
All:	Our hands clap the honor of your presence. (*Clap, clap.*) Our hearts and bodies jump with joy. *(Clap, clap.)* You blow our minds by singing over us. (*Clap, clap.*) Jesus. (*Clap, clap, clap.*) Amen. (*Clap, clap, clap.*)

ADVENT: WEEK 4A

Marketplace Praise

Genesis 24:34–38, 42–49, 58–67; Song of Songs 2:8–13; Romans 7:15–25a; Matthew 11:16–19, 25–30

All: We want it documented. As servants of our master, Christ, we will record all the acts of your great love and grace. We will turn them into songs of praise.

Women: With grateful thanks, we acknowledge that no one knows the Father except through Jesus, his Son.

Men: Jesus has broken the dominance of sin in our lives. Through his saving love, we are privileged to be embraced by Father, Son, and Spirit.

Left: Sin numbs us to doing good and strands us in the marketplace of self-interest, fixated with market share, market growth, and market dividends.

Right: Without grace, we are disorientated, and we keep doing the things we hate. But we know what is good: to love you and seek justice for the poor. But sin keeps taking the lead, locking us in step with the world.

All: As servants of our master, Christ, we proclaim that his name is above all names. We give thanks to our Lord, who redeems us from sin. His grace resuscitates us from this misery. The singing season has come.

Women: In the marketplace, we play the flute and sing of your great love. Show this world afresh the arrival of your presence as the Christ child.

Advent: Week 4A

Men: In the marketplace, we play a mournful song of the suffering sacrifice that Christ made for our sin. Break this world open like fallow ground so that all who struggle will find rest in Christ alone.

Left: We join the mournful song with the hope of resurrection light. You set us free from the prison of sin and death. In Christ, the Son, we are delivered and free.

Right: "Put on my yoke and learn from me," our master calls.[1] In his humble and gentle goodness, we find rest for weary souls and receive the fragrance of life anew.

All: So leap over mountains, bound over hills. In the cross, God's love is forever secure. Rise up to sing praise in marketplaces near and far. Today, let the fruit of his grace blossom into glorious shouts of praise.

---

1. Matt 11:29.

ADVENT: WEEK 4B

A Christmas Alphabet of Praise

Micah 5:2–5a; Psalm 80:1–7; Hebrews 10:5–10; Luke 1:39–55

Adult	All praise to God incarnate, who is enfleshed as Christ, his son.
Child	Bow down and worship the child who is King. Praise his name forever.
Adult	Come and adore him, Christ our Savior.
Child	Dew on the ground refreshes our memory of your love for the world.
Adult	Everyone is blessed through Mary's advent child.
Child	From ancient of days comes the child who makes all jump for joy.
Adult	God blesses all through Mary's Christ child.
Child	His face shines with the glory of the father. We bring the thanks of people who have been saved.
Adult	In the human form of a son, God is fully with us. Amen, amen!
Child	Can we see Jesus in Mary's arms as a body that will be broken for all?
Adult	Kindness, all yours, will wipe away our tears. Your presence in love will restore our enemies as neighbors. We give you praise.
Child	Love so longed for comes at Bethlehem's birth cry. We share the gasp of joy.

Advent: Week 4B

Adult	Mary, from your obedience, the new dawn of salvation has arrived. With you, all the lowly are lifted up.
Child	Now in our generation, we praise God from the depths of who we are. Jesus, Jesus, you are with us today.
Adult	Only you, God, the Father who sends the Son and the Spirit, can scatter those with arrogant thoughts and proud imaginations. Hosanna, again and again.
Child	Promises to Abraham are secured in this holy child. *Hallel* and *hallel*.
Adult	Questions are answered when your people are filled with the Holy Spirit. The loud cheers of the universe declare this as your plan.
Child	Rejoice and rejoice. The mighty one, our God, has done great things out of Bethlehem.
Adult	Sing and dance, this is the day of the blessed Christ child.
Child	The time has come, the old makes way for the new and becomes true for each generation. Praise God.
Adult	Under God's favor, the powerful are pulled away from their thrones while you lift up the lowly.
Child	Voices of joy sing your praise because in Bethlehem's babe, your power is shown to all who will see.
Adult	We wait this Advent day to see the hungry filled with good things.
Child	Exalt and shout hosanna, the great shepherd of the sheep is born in a manger.
Adult	Your love comes down at Christmas. We praise you, Lord, that from Bethlehem, you come out to us.
Child	Zoom, bang, and clash—God shows mercy to everyone at Christmas!

CHRISTMAS EVE

Holy Splendor Praise

Isaiah 9:2–7; Psalm 96; Titus 2:11–14; Luke 2:1–14

All stand.

All: Holy splendor, holy night. Praise the Lord, he has sent a great light.

Left: Holy splendor, holy night. Most wonderful counselor, his justice and righteousness roll down forever.

Right: Holy splendor, holy night. Mary has birthed the child of Jehovah and good news is told to the world.

Left: Holy splendor, holy night. Eternal father and prince of peace, we sing a new song to bless your name.

Right: Holy splendor, holy night. While shepherds shake and angels proclaim, this baby is wrapped with redemption's fame.

All sit.

All: *(Clap, clap, clap.)* All the people of earth are walking in darkness. Praise the Lord, he has sent a great light.

Left: All the people of earth are walking in darkness—so many trampled by warrior boots and blood-soaked garments. In distress, we barely speak.

Right: Though the people of earth are walking in darkness, a baby is born who will shatter this yoke. The zeal of God has become our hope.

Left: All the people of earth are walking in darkness—lawless behavior, gossip, theft, backchat, rejection, and bad things to say.

Right: Though the people of earth are walking in darkness, this babe is good news. Stand back, God's grace is appearing to remedy our blues.

All stand.

All: *(Clap, clap, clap.)* Holy splendor, holy night. The grace of God is carried on shouts of delight!

Left: Holy splendor, holy night. The Lord is coming to snuggle and rest while a dawn is unfolding on sin and despair.

Right: Holy splendor, holy night. Rejoice and roar with this marginal babe, for the good news of Jesus is a celebration sure.

Left: Holy splendor, holy night. Shepherds were blindsided by an angelic voice. The trees joined the shouts with full song of joy.

Right: Holy splendor, holy night. This Bethlehem stable is no scene of fake news. Come adore your Savior, Christ is the Lord.

All: Share the news of his salvation every day! *(Clap clap.)*

Left: *(Clap clap.)* Holy splendor, and glory to God.

Right: *(Clap clap.)* Holy night, peace to those in the light.

All: *(Clap clap.)* Yes, what a night!

Prayers for the Season of Christmastide

CHRISTMAS DAY A

Prayer in the Name of Jesus

Micah 5:2–5a; Psalm 80:1–7; Colossians 3:12–17; Luke 2:41–52

Leader:	We gather as a people chosen by God to put on Christ. Jesus, born as an insignificant one, now finds God's favor. Bethlehem, join our praise, for your name is now great throughout the earth.
People:	We are amazed that the ancient of days has become one of us. When we cried out, "wake up your power, Lord," humbly you came.[1] As the "one of peace," we invite you to direct our hearts.[2]
Leader:	Lord, make your face to shine on us today. Feed your people with bread made from the tears of the cross.[3] Jesus, we surrender all.
People:	In the name of Jesus, we bring praise into the Father's house. Bind us in unity, and through the peace of Christ, make us one.
Leader:	Jesus, you ask us, "why are you looking for me?"[4] We come to confess the darkness of our secular world. We confess our struggle to forgive the sins of others against us. We confess our lack of wisdom and empty visions.

1. Ps 80:2.
2. Mic 5:5.
3. Ps 80:5.
4. Luke 2:47.

Prayers for the Season of Christmastide

People: We are a blessed people because you have forgiven us. As your holy and loved ones, your desire is for us to "put on Christ."[5] We put on his compassion, kindness, humility, gentleness, and patience. Hallelujah!

Leader: Today we give ourselves to Christ, the one born in Bethlehem. We accept the encouragement to put on love. In season and out of season, we are committed to do everything in the name of Jesus, our newborn King.

People: With delight, we proclaim the majestic, humble name of Jesus. Today we remember your cross-shaped love. As we live forward, help us keep our promise to do all in the name of Jesus.

All: Greet one another in the peace of Christ, the newborn King!

---

5. Col 3:12.

CHRISTMAS DAY B

Heavy Lifting: Praise to the God with Us

Psalm 148; Isaiah 63:7–9; Hebrews 2:10–18; Matthew 2:13–23

All: Hallelujah in the highest. We who are close to Jesus are messengers of the good news. We praise God for sending his son!

Children (with leader): God, thank you. You are here with your children. We sing with joy for Bethlehem's baby!

Women: Wide as the oceans, high as the heavens, may all creation—all creatures great and small—praise God for his great favor. We praise the name of Jesus!

Men: Over the mountains, through the valleys and plains, may our leaders and kings, all young and old praise the one through whom everything exists. On this Christmas day, we praise the name of Jesus!

Children (with leader): God, you speak, and life appears. You arrange the ecosystems of our planet. You do the math that allows you to set the laws of gravity, motion, and light which govern the universe.

Women: The chorus of creation bears witness to your love. Your angels meet with us in dreams to strengthen our hope. Yet when we are distressed, you weep, even on this joyful Christmas day.

Men: From greatness, your son was born into uncertainty and endured suffering to pioneer salvation for the world. As recipients of the mystery of your grace, we shout with joy to the world on this Christmas day.

All: From Bethlehem, you stand by us in our temptation, and your grace wipes away our sins. You do all the heavy lifting in the most amazing of start-ups! Come, let us adore you! Glory to God in the highest!

CHRISTMASTIDE: WEEK 1A

A New Year Blessing

Psalm 147:12–20; Jeremiah 31:7–14; John 1:10–18; Ephesians 1:3–14

Leader: Bless the God and Father of our Lord Jesus Christ

People: God chose us in Christ through his amazing grace. We are God's adopted children through Jesus, the Messiah.

Leader: Bless God, the Creator of all, whose word makes the winds blow, the waters to flow, spreads the snow, scatters hail like crumbs, and then calls both to melt away.

People: We cry out for release from pandemic fever and from the wild spread of contagion. We remind you of your imagination, your calling us together as a new creation to be holy and blameless in your presence. O gracious one, this was in your mind well before the world as we know it.

Leader: Bless the God whose design is hidden in Christ, who plans to bring "all things" together in Christ.[1] To you be honor and glory.

People: From the fullness of Jesus, we testify that we have received grace upon grace. Shower our world with this breathtaking truth. Drench your people with love so that we can serve you, by your Holy Spirit.

Leader: Bless our God—Father, Son, and Spirit—who lavishes gifts upon us. When we are scattered, you bring us home rejoicing.

---

1. Eph 1:10.

People:	These troubled times are never far away from our thoughts. Deliver our world from this plague. Sustain our hope in this new year. Re-energize our health planners, scientists, and health workers for challenges ahead. Comfort all who are broken-hearted and distressed in any way. Through the power of the Spirit, fill your people with the compassion and power to serve.
Leader:	Bless our God, who turns mourning into dancing. In the power of your Spirit, make us watchmen for your salvation. Prepare us to be the ones who join the gospel shout of victory over sin, disease, despair, and death itself.
People:	Our delight is to know your presence as the Holy Spirit. Mold us and reshape our lives as sisters and brothers of Jesus. We remain open to the outpouring of your wisdom and understanding in our lives together. In the hope we share in Christ, we look forward to the blessings of a New Year.
Leader:	May the Lord of principalities and powers, empires and rulers, and all creation bless you. (*All clap.*) May the triune God, who in goodness accomplishes everything in his design plan, keep you in this time of distress. (*All raise hands.*) May God, whom we know in Christ, make his face to shine upon you. (*All wave and cheer.*)
All:	And may God grant us all in the year ahead the blessing of his peace. (*All pass the peace of Christ.*)

CHRISTMASTIDE: WEEK 1B

A New Year's Prayer

Ecclesiastes 3:1–13; Psalm 8; Revelation 21:1–6a; Matthew 25:31–46

Leader: At the beginning of this New Year, we praise your blessed name, O God, which is majestic in all the earth. Through your son, Jesus, you are making all things new.

All: We worship you, God, whose fingerprints are on every aspect of creation. You have mandated our responsibility for creation care.

Women: We love you, Lord. In your mindfulness, you care for us and have crowned us in glory and honor.

Men: In this New Year, we recognize your gift of time—past, present, and future. Keep us mindful that you have set in motion a new heaven and a new earth.

Leader: Alpha and Omega, author of all seasons, we celebrate your love for our world, which wipes away our tears and comforts us in our pain, sorrow, grief, and death. We are truly blessed.

All: As we live through the changes and challenges of our time, we recognize that you have ordained seasons to be born and to die, to plant and to pluck, to weep and to laugh, to embrace and to refrain from embracing. Our cry, Lord, is for you to restore pleasure to our toil so that we can eat and drink with joy.

Prayers for the Season of Christmastide

Women: Lord, fill our hearts with your love and compassion. Motivate us to feed the hungry, to bring drink to the thirsty, and to welcome the stranger among us, especially those seeking refuge. Open our ears to hear the cries of suffering and to respond.

Men: Lord, fill our hearts with your love and compassion. Motivate us to clothe the naked, to lead the homeless to shelter, and to visit the sick and imprisoned from our community. Open our ears to hear the cries of suffering and to respond.

Leader: At the start of this new year, we confess that we often fail to recognize the majesty of your great love in Christ. Forgive us and help us remember that you are making all things new. As we move forward into the new year, make us a welcoming community of faith by your Spirit.

All: Amen.

Prayers for the Season after Epiphany

SEASON AFTER EPIPHANY: WEEK 1A

Resolution Praise

Isaiah 60:1–16; Psalm 148; Galatians 4:4–7; Luke 2:22–40

Leader: Praise God, our Creator, who spoke and it came to be. Praise God, our sustainer, redeemer, and friend.

People: Our worship starts with caring for your creation. We resolve to be wholehearted stewards of the gifts of the cosmos and the teeming life of the earth.

Leader: Praise God, whose name is over all and whose majesty is far greater than the glory of creation.

People: We acknowledge our part in your created wonder. We share the delight of angels. We resolve to join with all creation to bring you praise.

Leader: Praise God—Father, Son, and Spirit—who sustains the integrity of all who are close to him.

People: We resolve to lift up our heads and see your glory in our present time.

Leader: Praise the Lord, whose light has come into our darkness through Jesus. His cross and resurrection radiate glory into the world.

People: We resolve to worship you with our whole selves. We open our hearts to receive your presence and to be moved by your action as you gather your people together in the splendor of your house.

Prayers for the Season after Epiphany

Leader: Praise our most merciful God, the Creator of the rugged mountains, sweeping plains, and wetlands teeming with diversity. God alone is the hope of the creation and all the nations of the earth.

People: From the shelter of your wings, we resolve to sing of your compassion and to shout out the glory of your name.

Leader: Praise the Lord, who will lead us by the Spirit into the paths of peace.

People: We resolve to live in anticipation of your kingdom coming by taking up our cross and following Jesus, our Lord.

Leader: All praise to our compassionate God, who consoles us in our suffering and loneliness. Our Savior's door is always open and welcoming.

People: We resolve to live out of our identity as your adopted children. We are at home in your redeeming love. We worship your mighty name.

All: We resolve to live as heirs of the kingdom, growing, serving, and praising Jesus with our whole hearts. Amen.

SEASON AFTER EPIPHANY: WEEK 1B

Anticipation Praise

Isaiah 63:7–9; Psalm 148; Hebrews 2:10–18; Matthew 2:13–23

All:	Hallelujah! We bring the new year's praise.
	We recount your faithful actions, Lord.
Children:	We bring the happy praise of children, who know your love.
Women:	The past, present, and future belong to you, God.
	Jesus, you have been with us since Bethlehem.
	We look through your love and mercy for the redemption of all things.
Men:	We join in this song of new year praise with all your messengers—
	earth, moon, and stars,
	fire, smoke, and stormy winds,
	hail and snow,
	birds, animals, and sea monsters.
	With all that exists, we shout, "hallelujah!"
All:	You have remained with us in times of distress.
	Your compassion and affection galvanize our praise and hope for the coming year.
Children:	We bring playful delight and cuddly pets to share this praise.
Women:	By your life, death, and resurrection, sweet Jesus,
	you are leading your people to your Father's glory.
Men:	We celebrate as we gather without fear or favor at the meal you have prepared for us.

Prayers for the Season after Epiphany

All: We receive the bread and wine from you, Christ, the most merciful and faithful high priest.

Children: We remember, Jesus, that your parents ran with you for their lives.
Thank you for protecting us.
We bring praise without fear into this new year.

Women: Lord, we praise you as members of your family in Jesus. Thank you for your embrace, which sets us free from our fears and disappointments. We resolve to serve you alone as we enter this new year.

Men: Amidst the struggle and evil threats in our world, accept our praise as members of your family in Jesus. We resolve to follow the steps of Jesus and to remember his life, death, and resurrection for the world.
Fill us with joy in the baptism of the Spirit.

All: From a world in motion, we bring new year praise to God, the Father, Son, and Spirit.
In this new year, may we center our anticipation in you as we feed on your word and as we drink from your enduring love. Amen!

SEASON AFTER EPIPHANY: WEEK 2A

A People Happy to Praise!

Genesis 1:1–5; Psalm 29; Acts 19:1–7; Mark 1:4–11

Children:	Father God, you were happy when Jesus came to dwell with us—and we are happy, too.
All:	*(Clap clap.)*
Adults:	Loving God, your happiness is infectious. As disciples of Jesus, we are bursting with joy as we witness our changing hearts and lives.
All:	*(Clap clap.)*
Children:	Wonderful God, you were happy at the time of creation. We delight in your good world, too.
All:	*(Clap clap.)*
Adults:	Creator God, you hovered over the chaos of matter. Through the Spirit, you spoke, and light shone in the darkness. We praise you for the goodness of your world!
All:	*(Clap clap.)*
Children:	Mighty God, you have a big, strong, majestic voice. When we worry, help us remember that your voice can shake the world.
All:	*(Clap clap.)*
Adults:	Sovereign God, you are Lord of all. You sit above the chaos of life and speak peace to all who follow your son. You calm our fears and stir the meek to shout, "glory."
All:	*(Clap clap.)*

Prayers for the Season after Epiphany

Children: Merciful God, we are happy because day and night, the light of Jesus shines on us.

All: *(Clap clap.)*

Adults: Most powerful God, we bow down and acknowledge your glory. When you fill us with your Spirit, we are delirious with praise.

All: *(Clap clap.)*

Children: Comforter God, you come to us like a gentle dove and fill our hearts with your love.

All: *(Clap clap.)*

Adults: Generous God, thank you for your gift of forgiveness through Jesus. We are happy to follow him and are grateful for the gift of your Spirit.

All: *(Clap clap.)* Today we sing, "It is Jesus we love." We don't need to worry, because we are happy to praise you alone. *(Clap, clap, clap.)*

SEASON AFTER EPIPHANY: WEEK 2B

Praise for God's Strong Hand of Love

Jonah 3:1–5, 10; Psalm 62:5–12; 1 Corinthians 6:12–20; John 1:43–51

People:	God's strong hand rescues us from the tangles of sin. God's gracious love disempowers all evil.
Leader:	God's word comes as judgement upon those who turn toward evil and reap the wages of sin.
People:	God's strong hand is our rock, salvation, and refuge. God's love has brought us back to life from death. As followers of Jesus, the rhythms of praise go with us.
Leader:	God's word comes as judgement upon those who weaponize their bodies and hand over their autonomy to the power of sin.
People:	God's strong hand reorientates us to a place of rest, where we will not be shaken. God's love transforms us to become servants of righteousness and holiness. As followers of Jesus, a harmony of praise draws us together.
Leader:	God's word comes as judgement upon those who trust in violence, commit robbery, and set their hearts on wealth.
People:	God's strong hand delivers us from evil and establishes our integrity as we entrust our lives to his grace. God's love opens space for us to pour out our hearts before him and also marks us for service. As followers of Jesus, a chant of praise accompanies us.
Leader:	God's word comes as judgement upon those who pull others down and set snares of deception.

People: God's strong hand sustains the weak, who are like "a leaning wall" and "a broken-down fence."[1] God's love generates hope within us, and his grace renders sin powerless over us. As followers of Jesus, we erupt with cheers of praise.

All: We praise God, whose word always comes a second time. As followers of Jesus, we are ready to see your strong hands of love renewing the world.

---

1. Ps 62:3.

SEASON AFTER EPIPHANY: WEEK 3A

For Pleasing Praise from Your People

Nehemiah 8:1–3; Psalm 19; 1 Corinthians 12:12–31a; Luke 4:4–21

All: Gracious Lord, let the words of our mouths and the meditation of our hearts be pleasing to you, our rock and redeemer.

Leader: Lord, we are a starstruck people. Your glory is on tour in the skies, night and day. You pull life together and reveal your love throughout creation.

Women: Yet we live such partial and piecemeal lives. Today, we come together as brothers and sisters, longing to fix our eyes on you and your love, Jesus, so that we can live a large and integrated life of faith.

Men: Yet we confess that the temptation for power, fame, and pleasure is always near. Today, we come together, arm in arm in our confession, longing to worship you with the whole of our lives so that you, Jesus, have the final say.

Leader: Lord, we are a people who love to hear your word, and so we strain our ears for your direction from Scripture. Your life maps offer good news for our lives, showing us the way towards freedom and joy.

Men: Yet we tempt you God, by our attraction to so many things. We have constructed idols of food, technology, financial security, entertainment, and our own pleasure. Today, the cry of our hearts is to see Jesus and to repent and hear the good news afresh. Release us from our burdened and battered lives and set our feet on your righteous road.

Women: Yet the world around us is chaotic, and we are often afraid to take up your cross and follow you wherever you lead us, Jesus. Today, we proclaim that you are the living word, the one on whom the Spirit rests. Remind us that we do not walk alone, for you have sent your Spirit as our comforter and guide.

All: Gracious Lord, let the words of our mouths and the meditation of our hearts be pleasing to you, our rock and redeemer.

SEASON AFTER EPIPHANY: WEEK 3B

Praise from the Darkness and Praise from the Light

Psalm 40; Isaiah 49:1–7; Matthew 4:12–23; 1 Corinthians 1:1–9

Leader: We declare your faithfulness and salvation, even when we find ourselves weak, needy, and stuck in the mud of life.

People: You are our redeemer from the darkness of poor health, frailty, uncertainty, sin, and despair. Though we can be blindsided by the confidence of the proud and those who spread fake news about you, we will praise you for listening to our cries, lifting us up, and restoring new songs of joy in our lives.

Leader: We declare your amazing grace through Jesus Christ. By grace, you lean toward us with affection and hold nothing back from us. As we wait for Jesus to be revealed in the world, our only hope is in you.

People: You put our feet on solid ground and lead us into the light. We declare that we are willing to change our hearts and lives and to do your will. May your kingdom come!

All: We praise you for your loyal compassion.
We praise you for your great and self-giving love.
We praise you for making us holy in Jesus.
We praise you for the plans you have for us.
We praise you for calling us to walk as your people through times of darkness and light.
Amen!

SEASON AFTER EPIPHANY: WEEK 4A

Praise for God's Word in our Mouth

Deuteronomy 18:15–30; Psalm 111;
1 Corinthians 8:1–13; Mark 1:21–28

Leader:	There is one God, the Father. All things come from him, and we belong to him.
All:	This is God's word in our mouth.
Leader:	There is one Lord, Jesus Christ. All things exist through him, and we live through him.
All:	This is God's word in our mouth.
Left:	But not everyone knows this, for knowledge makes some people arrogant, and yet love builds people up.
All:	This is God's word in our mouth.
Right:	When we ask, "Jesus, what have you to do with us?" you teach us that if we love God, we are known by God.[1]
All:	This is God's word in our mouth.
Leader:	Jesus, the holy one of Nazareth, is with us. Of him, God says, "I will put my words in his mouth."[2]
All:	This is God's word in our mouth.
Leader:	There is only one God, who is "famous for his wondrous works."[3]
All:	This is God's word in our mouth.

1. Mark 1:24.
2. Deut 18:18.
3. Ps 111:2.

Left:	We thank God for his mercy and compassion in days past and in our present distress.
All:	This is God's word in our mouth.
Right:	We thank God for his word, which is where wisdom begins. At God's word, all evil is dismissed.
All:	God's word in our mouth is praise forever!

SEASON AFTER EPIPHANY: WEEK 4B

Lasting Praise

Deuteronomy 18:15–20; Psalm 111;
1 Corinthians 8:1–13; Mark 1:21–28

Leader: We are followers of Jesus, the holy one from God. Some believe in idols in heaven and on earth, for not everyone knows that there is only one God.

People: Through Jesus, our praise to God lasts forever. Hallelujah!

Leader: We are followers of God, whose handiworks are honesty, justice, and righteousness.

People: Through Jesus, God has sent us redemption. Hallelujah!

Leader: We are followers of "one God, the father. All things come from him, and we belong to him. And there is one Lord, Jesus Christ. All things exist through him, and we live through him."[1]

People: Through Jesus, we can embrace lasting praise. *(Clap clap.)*

Leader: Though knowledge can lead to arrogance, the willingness to praise God is the beginning of wisdom.

People: Through Jesus, we can embrace lasting praise. *(Clap clap.)*

Leader: The Spirit of love builds us up, and when we seek to love God, we discover that God already knows us.

---

1. 1 Cor 8:6.

People	Through Jesus, we can embrace lasting praise. *(Clap clap.)*
Leader:	Praise God for the word of the Lord! Praise the Lord for his magnificent works! Praise Jesus, who is full of mercy and compassion!
People:	Through Jesus, we embrace joyful praise. *(Clap clap.)*
Leader:	Because the kingdom of God is among us in Jesus, we can't hold back our praise.
People:	Through Jesus, we can praise the Father *(Clap clap.)*
Leader:	In the unity of Father, Son, and Spirit, there is only one God—and so we are compelled to offer a harmony of praise.
People:	Through the Spirit, we can praise God forever. *Clap clap.)*
Leader:	Praise the creating and redeeming God, whose enduring presence among us is a lasting treasure.
People:	Through Jesus, we embrace joyful praise. *(Clap clap.)*
Leader:	"There is one God, the father. All things come through him, and we belong to him. And there is one Lord, Jesus Christ. All things exist through him, and we live through him."[2]
People:	Hallelujah! Hallelujah! *(Clap clap, applause.)*

---

2. 1 Cor 8:6.

SEASON AFTER EPIPHANY: WEEK 5A

In Praise of the God who Comes

2 Kings 2:1–12; Psalm 50:1–6; 2 Corinthians 4:3–6; Mark 9:2–9

Children: God is coming, and he won't keep quiet.

Adults: We gather and come as your faithful. We echo the call of your love in shouts of acclamation and praise.

Children: God is coming, and he won't keep quiet.

Adults: Lord, you are a bright light shining out in the dark. The skies proclaim your beauty, and the whole creation gives you praise.

Children: God is coming, and he won't keep quiet.

Adults: Eternity surrounds you, and your glory emanates from the face of Jesus. We bring you new covenant praise and shout, "Glory to God!"

Children: God is coming, and he won't keep quiet.

Adults: Though we live in the world, surrounded by struggles and distractions, we proclaim that Jesus Christ is Lord. Your light surrounds us like fire. In mercy, receive our sacrifice of praise.

Children: God is coming, and he won't keep quiet.

Adults: Though our days are numbered, and windstorms and firestorms ravage the earth, your voice calls out, "bring my faithful to me."[1] We confess that we do not always

---

1. Ps 50:5.

Season after Epiphany: Week 5A

	heed your voice and humbly ask you to accept our penitent praise.
Children:	God is coming, and he won't keep quiet.
Adults:	Jesus, you alone can see the bright hope of salvation for the whole world. Shine your light into places of darkness and soften the hearts of those who have shut themselves off from your love so that all can behold the glory of God.
Children:	God is coming and he won't keep quiet.
Adults:	Awesome Creator, your glory transfigures all darkness. Thank you for putting the light of Christ in our hearts and for sending your son, whom you love, into the world.
All:	Jesus, we are listening for you. You will never leave us alone. And when you come, no one will keep quiet. Hallelujah!

SEASON AFTER EPIPHANY: WEEK 5B

Praise to Jesus

Exodus 34:29–35; Psalm 99; 2 Corinthians 3:12–4:2; Luke 9:28–34

All: Through the mystery of the cloud of unknowns, we praise the great and awesome name of Jesus.

Left: You are exalted over all the peoples, and so we humbly worship at your footstool.

Right: You are the lover of justice, and your commandments are wrapped in covenanting love.

Left: You have shown your people the way of equity, justice, and righteousness through your servants Moses and Jakob. In Jesus, your equity, justice, and righteousness comes afresh.

Right: You are our forgiving Lord, so we honor you and shout out your praise.

Left: Sourced in your mystery, your commands and covenantal rules of engagement are now brought to life in Jesus. Give us hope so that we can live boldly as a people who have been led out of slavery and fear. We surrender all to you.

Right: As we come into the mystery of your presence, shine, Jesus, and fill our hearts with your glory. Remove all echoes of slavery and fear from our lives.

Left: Sweet Jesus, you pull aside the veil of sin, rebelliousness, ignorance, and fear.

Season after Epiphany: Week 5B

Right: We heed the father's voice, saying, "This is my son, my chosen, listen to him."[1]

Left: Christ, we have tasted your mercy, and we accept with open hearts your cross-shaped love into our lives.

Right: As we listen for your voice, Jesus, we are transformed by grace into your likeness.

All: We embrace the deep mystery of your self-giving love. By the power of your Spirit, set us free to follow and listen for your voice, for the sake of the world. Amen.

---

1. Luke 9:35.

SEASON AFTER EPIPHANY: WEEK 6A

We will Sing your Praise

Psalm 138; Isaiah 6:1–8; Luke 5:1–11; 1 Corinthians 15:1–11

All:	Father, Son, and Holy Spirit, the whole earth is full of your glory. Refocus our minds on the good news of the grace of Jesus Christ.
Women:	We humbly present ourselves for your service and sing your praise before the power of individualism.
Men:	Your faithfulness gives us our daily bread, and so we sing your praise before the power of consumerism.
All:	Your steadfast love sustains us, and so we sing your praise before the power of globalization.
Women:	You call us to work hard for justice and to regard the lowly, so we sing your praise before the power of inequality and greed.
Men:	We recognize the sin of intolerance in our hearts, and so we sing your praise before the power of racism.
All:	We recognize all the ways we have corrupted your good and fragile creation, and so we cry out for mercy and sing your praise before all the powers that are seeking to exploit your creation.
Women:	We believe that Christ died for our sins, was buried, rose on the third day, and continues to appear to us today, and so we sing your praise before the disenchanted power of secularism.

Season after Epiphany: Week 6A

Men: We feel the suffering and lost crowds of humanity pressing against us at every side, and so we sing your praise before the power of skepticism.

All: Lord, renew our lives and buffer us from the powers of our age. We have worked hard and long for your gospel. Calm our fears just as you stilled the storm on the Sea of Galilee so that we will be overcome by the power of your grace as we continue to sing your praise through all the storms of life. Amen.

SEASON AFTER EPIPHANY: WEEK 6B

A Song of Praise by Faith

Genesis 12:1–4(a); Psalm 121; Romans 4:1–5, 13–17; Matthew 17:1–9

All kneel.

All:	God beyond the cloud of unknowing, we come in humility to bring you praise. We have heard your calling to serve the coming kingdom and are ready to proclaim your name throughout the world.
Men:	By faith, we are members of the genealogy of Abraham.
Women:	By faith, we are the body of Christ.

All sit.

All:	God beyond the horizons of the mountains, seas, and plains, we praise you for being our protector. We have heard your promise never to let our feet slip from faith.
Men:	By faith, protect your church from evil as we remember Jesus in the breaking of bread.
Women:	By faith, protect your church as we share the cup of wine and remember your life given for us.

All stand.

All:	Like Abraham, we walk by faith as we seek to follow your call to become a blessing for our world. We are inspired by the love we see between the Father and the Son.
Men:	By faith, we go out under your covering through the ever-giving love of Jesus.

Season after Epiphany: Week 6B

Women:	By faith, we serve without fear and celebrate our inheritance through grace.
	All stretch out arms.
All:	By faith, we sit at the feet of Jesus, the light of the world, and listen to his voice. Our hearts overflow with love and joy.
Men:	By faith, we rise up and proclaim our desire to serve you, Jesus, through your resurrection power.
Women:	As daughters of Abraham's faith, we are willing, to go out in love to serve wherever you lead us, Lord Jesus. As heirs of Abraham's faith, we bring praise and glory to God the Father, Son, and Spirit.

All sit for silent prayer.

Leader:	For the people of Harran, Abraham's hometown.
All:	*(Pray in silence.)*
Leader:	For the people of Syria and Turkey, where the apostle Paul faithfully proclaimed the gospel.[1]
All:	*(Pray in silence.)*

---

1. Gal 1:21.

Prayers for the Season of Lent

ASH WEDNESDAY

From Ashes to Songs of Praise

Isaiah 58:1–12, Psalm 51:1–17;
2 Corinthians 5:20b–6:10, Matthew 6:1–6, 16–21

Leader: We practice self-delusion when our self-talk suggests that we are free of sin. We all miss the mark. The fault line of good and evil gapes within us and all around us. Receive the ashes of our repentance as humble songs of praise. Today we fast from our arrogant ways and seek your forgiveness.

People: We want our confession to run deep. We admit that we are good at the show, the appearance of living a spiritual life and doing good deeds. Through these signs, we suggest to the world that our desire is to be close to you. Yet the truth is, we are doing all these things for our own benefit. In your faithful love, Lord, have mercy on us.

Leader: In mercy, wipe the slate clean of all our false pretenses. We tend to slip and slide into quarrels, greedy behaviors, and violent actions and thoughts. Oppression is within our reach. Pride threatens to bang down the door of your grace.

People: Our sins are at the front of our mind, and so we seek your great compassion. Forgive us for our self-serving propaganda. Free our hearts from the bondage of self-interest.

Prayers for the Season of Lent

Leader: Today is the day of God's salvation, when God's light can shine into our darkness. Today God is wiping away our dishonor and reorienting us so that we can work with Jesus for justice in joy and peace. This is a new day soaked in praise.

People: Lord, we do not want to cut corners in our relationship with you. You desire for us to endure problems, disasters, and stressful situations with the integrity of repentance and surrender. We desire to praise your name and let love transform our hearts. Today we give you our hallelujah!

Leader: Already your transforming grace is changing our hearts and lives. We are ready to open our lips and sing to you our chorus of praise.

People: We want to sing your song of love as we serve the hungry and afflicted. We want to sing your song of freedom as we walk with victims of injustice. We want to dance and sing with joy as we see the poor embrace the good news of your love and compassion for all.

All: Amen.

LENT: WEEK 1A

Lonely Heart Praise

Isaiah 40:21–31; Psalm 147:1–11; 20c;
1 Corinthians 9:16–23; Mark 1:29–39

Left:	God of our horizons, you sustain us on the journey of life. Help us find comfort in our long days of isolation and loneliness by singing your praise. Hallelujah!
Right:	God of our freedom, we are trying to make sense of our place in the world so that we can praise you with joy regardless of the circumstances of our life. Your love enlivens us, because we know you have the power to raise us up so we can serve you in praise!
Left:	When we think we are alone, our hearts break, but when we gather in the power of your love, your Spirit renews our strength. When we walk alone, we become fatigued and exhausted, but your Holy Spirit gives us courage and emboldens us to give you praise! When we walk with you, we will never grow weary.
Right:	When we are isolated in sickness and we feel our fevers rising, you heal us in compassion. You raise us up us for service in your kingdom, Lord. Nothing compares with you!
Left:	Your word declares, "God helps the poor."[1] You heal the broken-hearted and set the oppressed free. You treasure those who honor you in their lives and through their praise.

---

1. Ps 147:6.

Right: Every lonely heart is searching for you, so bless all who wait for the emergence of your faithful love. Tend the earth, bring refreshing rain, and feed us so that we can give you praise.

Left: The world urges us to win and strive for the prize—military might, financial success, and fame. Alone, we remain empty, thirsting for your love. Head in our direction, Lord, and refresh and empower our lives so that we will be strengthened to bring you praise.

Right: When we are tempted to say, "my way is hidden from the Lord," or, "God ignores my predicament,"[2] lift our eyes to your skies. Reignite our vision so that we can see your creative power and your great strength, which has the mighty power to sustain us. You are our everlasting God. Hallelujah!

All: We want our lonely world to know that "those who hope in the Lord renew their strength. They fly up on wings like eagles."[3] Through his spirit, God revives the lonely and exhausted so that they can praise his name. For the sake of the gospel, Lord, hear our prayer and help us to give you beautiful praise. Amen!

---

2. Isa 40:27b.
3. Isa 40:31.

LENT: WEEK 1B

Praise of Delight and Eager Anticipation

Malachi 3:1–4; Psalm 24:7–10; Hebrews 2:14–18; Luke 2:22–40

People:	We who belong to the Lord gather in his presence. The paths are clear for us to delight in Jesus, who bears God's covenant of love to the whole world. Hallelujah!
Leader:	We are amazed that Christ has come among us to share our humanity, our flesh and blood, and to teach us how to reflect your glory.
Women:	We are eager to seek the Lord. We present ourselves as living sacrifices and seek to be led by the spirit. So come, Holy Spirit, rest on us!
Men:	We praise God, who makes us strong and wise in grace by the power of the Spirit. We proclaim that Jesus is Lord to everyone who is ready to hear.
People:	With delight, we confess our dedication to the way of Jesus. By your Spirit, reveal Jesus among us in the breaking of bread and the drinking of wine.
Leader:	As we share in the body and blood of Jesus, we acknowledge that he is our merciful and faithful high priest. He alone cancels our sins through his life, death, and resurrection. We anticipate all the blessings that God will pour out among us by his Spirit.
Women:	Surprise us with your refining presence, Lord. We desire the integrity of abiding in you!

Men: Surprise us with your cleansing, purifying presence, Lord. We want to present righteous offerings to you, the fruit of your grace among us.

People: Strong and powerful Lord, through your cross-shaped presence in the world, overturn the power of suffering and death and bring all principalities and powers into submission to your will. May the peace of your kingdom transform and heal all evil and violence in our world. Our anticipation and hope is centered in you, Father, Son, and Spirit. Hallelujah!

LENT: WEEK 2A

Praise in the Field of God's Dream

Isaiah 55:1–9; Psalm 63:1–8; 1 Corinthians 10:1–13; Luke 13:1–9

People: Today we gather to bless the Lord, whom we know as Father, Son, and Spirit. We give God our blessing, thanksgiving, and praise through the harmony of being in Christ. We celebrate together God's field of dreams.

Left: We had big plans. We preferred to be big spenders, to shop till we dropped, to grow our nest egg.

Right: We had big plans. We desired fine cuisine, the pleasures of wining and dining. Our fast-food hunger became an obsession.

Leader: God asks, "Why are you spending money on counterfeits? Why are fine foods and fast foods leaving you unsatisfied?"[1] God invites us to ponder his grace and to listen carefully to his plans.

People: Today we gather to bless the Lord, whom we know as Father, Son, and Spirit. We give God our blessing, thanksgiving, and praise through the harmony of being in Christ. We celebrate together God's field of dreams.

Left: We had big plans. We responded to the attraction of power. We strove to be top dog and to put others in their place. We happily did life our own way.

---

1. Isa 55:2.

Right:	We had big plans. We enjoyed the thrill of giving way to naughtiness. We wanted to demonstrate our prowess. Faithfulness and loyalty felt boring.
Leader:	God's plans come with a warning bell, for a day of judgement can catch us by surprise. He calls wicked ways and sinful schemes to account. He is ready to uproot all fruitless lives.
People:	Today we gather to bless the Lord, whom we know as Father, Son, and Spirit. We give God our blessing, thanksgiving, and praise through the harmony of being in Christ. We celebrate together God's field of dreams.
Left:	With parched hearts, we seek the Lord. Can God still color our world? The whispering in our hearts is a faithful call to run into his generous, forgiving arms.
Right:	With dry hearts, we return to the Lord. Our life seems to be running on empty. Will their still be room for his mercy? Is there still protection under her wings?
Leader:	The plans of the Lord outlast our sins and disloyalty. God's plan is for us to respond by faith to his salvation and liberation in Christ. Day and night we ponder God's goodness. As people fully satisfied by grace, we praise the Lord with joy on our lips.
People:	Today we gather to bless the Lord, whom we know as Father, Son, and Spirit. We give God our blessing, thanksgiving, and praise through the harmony of being in Christ. We celebrate together God's field of dreams.
Left:	God's plans are way beyond our wildest imagination. We cling to Christ in love, for he satisfies our whole being, body, heart, and lives. We drench Jesus with our praise, filled with wonder as we explore God's field of dreams.
Right:	We see God's plans in the glory and power of Christ, who was crucified and raised from the dead to liberate us from the power of sin so that we could walk in freedom. With arms outstretched, we burst with grateful joy as we dance in God's field of dreams.

Lent: Week 2A

Leader: Our thirst is quenched as we meditate on God's plans. The Lord's strong arm lifts us up when we are weakened by sin and indifference. Though our big plans have failed, God's plans surpass our expectations. The faithful loyalty of the Lord turns everything around, to the glory of his name.

All: Today we gather to bless the Lord, whom we know as Father, Son, and Spirit. We give God our blessing, thanksgiving, and praise through the harmony of being in Christ. We celebrate together God's field of dreams.

LENT: WEEK 2B

Hope in God, Who is Willing to Hear

Genesis 43:3–11, 15; Psalm 37:1–11, 39–40;
1 Corinthians 15:35–38, 42–50; Luke 6:27–38

Leader: Lord, our world is noisy with the twenty-four-seven entertainment and news cycles. Workplaces demand efficiencies that stretch us to the limits of our fatigue. Today we quiet down in your presence. We prayerfully and patiently listen for your voice. In hope, we bring you our prayer.

Women: Lord of love, our broken lives and relationships leave us angry and distressed. We need the gospel to bring us reconciliation and new hope so that we can trust in your love and do good.

Men: Lord of love, the spacious free life is centered in you. Restrain us when anger gets the better of us. When envy or obsessive thoughts about our neighbors' successes lead to sinful responses, help us turn to you. We anchor our true hope in your salvation.

Women: We are keeping nothing back, Lord. We open our lives to your scrutiny. Take us in all our weakness and raise us up through the resurrection power of Christ.

Men: Lord, you teach us to treat others the way we desire to be treated. We confess it is challenging to love our enemies, to turn the other cheek when violence comes, and to do good to those who hate us. Take our broken lives and raise us up through the power of our risen Lord.

Lent: Week 2B

Women: Father, Son, and Holy Spirit, you are a compassionate God. You validate the lives of all who love you, and you remain kind to the ungrateful and wicked.

Men: May the power of your love overflow in our lives so that we can cease to judge or condemn our neighbors.

Leader: As a seed dies so that it can rise again in new glory, Christ has died to share the glory of heaven with all who repent and believe. Lord, we affirm that you are our refuge in this time of isolation and distress. We commit to remain compassionate and hopeful as you hear our prayer. Amen.

LENT: WEEK 3A

Do Be Do Be Praise

Numbers 21:4–9; Psalm 107:1–3, 17–22;
Ephesians 2:1–10; John 3:14–21

All:	Do be do be, we are saved by grace through faith.
	Do be do be, our God is rich in mercy. (*Clap.*)
	Do be do be, God's gift of freedom and salvation is for all. Praise his name!
Left:	We often follow the rules of destructive spiritual power.
	We tend to do whatever feels good.
Right:	We are often tempted to become impatient on the road.
	We are a people who willingly complain about God.
Leader:	But give thanks to God, who is good.
	Give thanks to God, who loves the world
	Give thanks to the Father, who sent his only Son to save us.
All:	Do be do be, we are saved by grace through faith.
	Do be do be, our God is rich in mercy. (*Clap.*)
	Do be do be, God's gift of freedom and salvation is for all. Praise his name!
Left:	We often live in a spirit of disobedience to God's will.
	We are a people who moan in hard times and in confusion ask, "why did you save us?"[1]
Right:	We live with the consequences of our sinful ways.
	We lose our appetite for life and are attracted by death.

---

1. See Num 21:5.

Lent: Week 3A

Leader: But you are the God who saves us from despair.
For you give the command, and we are healed.
Your plan is for us to live the way of life so that in you, we can do good things.

All: Do be do be, we are saved by grace through faith.
Do be do be, our God is rich in mercy. (*Clap.*)
Do be do be, God's gift of freedom and salvation is for all. Praise his name!

Left: As we walk through desert times, we are tempted to think that you want to make us suffer and die.
As we focus on ourselves and what we can do, we are tempted to look elsewhere for salvation.

Right: We disconnect ourselves from your body, the broken bread of life.
We find ourselves in the pits, desperate for your salvation.

Leader: But you are our redeemer, and we are your "accomplishment, created in Christ Jesus to do good things."[2]

All: Do be do be, we are saved by grace through faith.
Do be do be, our God is rich in mercy. (*Clap.*)
Do be do be, God's gift of freedom and salvation is for all. Praise his name!

Left: Remind us that we don't posses grace on our own.
Remind us not to be proud of anything we do by your grace.

Right: Like Moses lifting up the snake in the wilderness to save the dying people,
we lift Jesus up so that we can be healed once more of the poisonous nature of sin.

Leader: For God gave us his son so that all who believe in his name will have eternal life.
And God is rich in mercy, for even while we are dead in sin, he brings us to life in Christ. Praise the name of Jesus!

---

2. Eph 2:10.

All: Do be do be, we are saved by grace through faith. Hallelujah!
Do be do be, our God is rich in mercy. Amen! (*Clap.*)
Do be do be, God's gift of freedom and salvation is for all. Praise his name!
To God be all glory and honor!
Amen! (*Clap clap.*) Amen! (*Clap, clap, clap.*)

LENT: WEEK 3B

We Cry, "Peace, Peace"

Deuteronomy 26:1–11; Psalm 91:1–2, 9–16; Romans 10:8b–13; Luke 4:1–13

Leader:	We gather as your devoted people, who know you as Father, Son, and Holy Spirit.
	We testify to your strong arm to save.
	We claim the promise of your word.
	We trust that you are with us in troubling times.
People:	Our faith in Christ has produced fruit in our lives.
	We bring the "praise of gratefulness" as we seek to live in faith, hope, and love.[1]
	You are our God, the one in whom we trust.
All:	We cry, "Peace, peace."
Leader:	Creator God, your gift of the earth is our inheritance.
	We offer up the grief and trouble of our community as we are swept along by floods and climate events.
	In your providence, we ask you not to discriminate.
	Hear our cry and help both the just and the unjust, the powerful and the weak.
People:	Saving God, the gift of life itself is our inheritance.
	We offer up the misery and oppression of our neighbors in _____.
	As the blood flows in these places, stretch out your strong arm and bring a just peace.
	Stretch out your compassionate hands and bring signs and wonders of reconciliation.

1. Deut 26:11.

All:	We cry, "Peace, peace."
Leader:	Healing God, you desire for no disease to take up residence in our homes.
	As we live within your shelter, offer us the protection of your shade.
	We cry out for the sick and sorrowing in your world, all who are struggling with the burden of afflictions.
	Ignite your promise to come quickly to help and heal.
People:	In the power of the Spirit, we call on your name.
	Sin leaves terrible stains, and so we cry for the deliverance of our world.
	May all confess with their mouths, "Jesus is Lord!"[2]
	May all trust in the power of the resurrected Christ to heal and renew the world.
All:	We cry, "Peace, peace."
Leader:	We confess our desire for power over the kingdoms of this world.
	We acknowledge our powerlessness in the face of the forces of nature.
	We recognize the ongoing threat of acute and chronic diseases.
	We humbly surrender to your words of comfort.
	Hold back these evils and carry us to the satisfaction of old age.
People:	Lord, hear our cries, shouts, pleas, and whimpers.
	You promise to give generously to all who call on your name.
	Answer us as we cry out for you to protect us and our world.
	In Christ, save us and restore your dignity in all humanity.
All:	We cry, "Peace, peace."

---

2. Rom 10:9.

LENT: WEEK 4A

Praying Together in the Cruciform Way

Exodus 20:1–17; Psalm 19; Corinthians 1:18–25; John 2:13–22

Leader:	Father, Son, and Spirit, you have created this world and its people in love.
Men:	We pray as gospel people, whose lives are being transformed because of your cross-shaped love for the world in Jesus.
Women:	We pray in the name of Jesus because after three days, he rose from the grave.
All:	Heaven declares your good work. The planets, stars, mountains, valleys, oceans, wetlands, deserts, and all the living creatures of this earth reveal the glory of your name.
Leader:	May the words of our mouth and the meditations of our hearts in this time of denial and fasting reflect your cross-shaped presence in this world, Lord Christ.
Men:	We recognize your image within us and accept the responsibility to steward all that you have given us.
Women:	We accept your charter to care for the earth against the forces of pollution, global warming, and shrinking biodiversity.
All:	We commit to work for peace, to engage in activities that will help restore your polluted creation, and to seek justice for the oppressed. With you, we hear the cries of the poor, the unborn, and all who live with unresolved suffering.

Prayers for the Season of Lent

Leader: You are our redeemer from the scourge of sin. Your instruction revives our very being. Your laws make our naivety wise. Your regulations gladden our hearts and give light to our eyes.

Men: We confess the reality of sin in our lives and the impact it is having in the world. We acknowledge the beauty of the law given to Moses and know that your will is for us to love you with our whole hearts, to turn away from other gods, and to refrain from worshipping idols.

Women: We embrace your law and will seek to honor your name and to remember the Sabbath and keep it holy.

All: We will write your law on our hearts and seek to honor our parents and all life. We will not commit adultery, steal from, or covet anything belonging to our neighbors, and we will not testify falsely against them.

Leader: We are set free from sin and the law through repentance and trust in the cross-shaped love of God in Christ.

Men: Our world sees God's self-giving love in the death of Jesus as scandalous.

Women: Our world sees God's self-giving love in the death of Jesus as foolish.

All: The self-giving love of God in Christ is not weakness, but demonstrates the redeeming power of the gospel for all. The cross is God's signature of love to our world.

Leader: May we live out of your resurrection power as we follow your calling for our lives today.

LENT: WEEK 4B

Standing Firm in the Love of God

Genesis 15:1–12, 17–18; Psalm 27;
Philippians 3:17—4:1; Luke 13:31–35

All stand.

All: We praise God—Father, Son, and Holy Spirit.
The embracing love of God is our shield.
The self-giving love of Jesus is our light and salvation.
The transforming love of the Spirit sustains our hope in times of trouble.

Left: We imitate the faith of our sisters and brothers who have been caught in the grip of peril and war, but have experienced your presence as a fortress, protecting their life.
They testify to your goodness in the land of the living.
We cry out for you to sustain their hearts of courage.

Right: We hope in your covenant love, which teaches us not to be afraid.
In times of trouble, strengthen the faith of your people.
Restrain those who are evildoers in our world.
You are a rock of safety for all who love you.

All sit.

All:	We praise you for demonstrating your love for the world by sending your Son.
	We confess that we have also been enemies of your cross-shaped love.
	By grace, sweep us under your wings.
	Hear our cry to protect those who are oppressed by their enemies.
Left:	We praise our risen Lord, who says to us, "do not be afraid."[1]
	Send the flaming torch of your Spirit to bring peace to places of terror and war.
	Come into our world, Lord Jesus, come.
Right:	We confess our faith in this troubling time as we are surrounded by violent accusers and false witnesses.
	Have mercy on us, Lord.
	Hear our cries for relief for the people of _____.
	Remember the land you have given all the people groups of the world.
	Come, Lord Jesus, come.

All stand.

All:	Risen Lord Jesus, be with your people. Heal us, protect us, and bring peace to your world.
Left:	The Lord is our light and our salvation. Should we fear anyone?[2]
	Transform our lives so that we can be peacemakers for the sake of your glorious Son.
Right:	We acknowledge that our citizenship comes from heaven.
	We humbly seek to live in the presence of your love forever.
	By your Spirit, empower us to love our enemies today and going forward.
All:	Amen.

1. Matt 14:27 (NRSV).
2. Ps 27:1.

LENT: WEEK 5A

Solidarity with Christ

Jeremiah 31:31–34; Psalm 119:9–16; Hebrews 5:5–10; John 12:20–33

All: The time is coming, Lord. With Christ, we must be buried and die, like a seed, so that we can become the fruit of your enduring love for the world.

Left: Having received Christ's salvation, we commit to follow Jesus wherever he is today. When he is deeply troubled, so are we. When he is glorified, you cover us with grace. We glorify and honor his name.

Right: On the cross, Jesus draws all people to himself through his obedience to his Father, even in suffering and death. With Jesus, we will rise as daughters and sons of our loving Father. The cross of Christ has the power to disarm all resistance to your grace.

All: The time is coming, Lord. With Christ, we must be buried and die, like a seed, so that we can become the fruit of your enduring love for the world.

Left: As you engrave your law on our hearts, we become your people. From the least to the greatest, we know you through Christ. Teach us your statutes so that we will not stray off course and sin. We bless the Lord and find solidarity with Christ.

Right: We seek you with our whole hearts, Lord. We examine your pathways and delight in your precepts. We rejoice that in following Jesus, we can come to know and be known by you, God. We bring our humble praise and find solidarity with Christ.

All: The time is coming, Lord. With Christ, we must be buried and die, like a seed, so that we can become the fruit of your enduring love for the world.

Left: When we love our own lives, we lose them, and so we surrender all to Jesus and find solidarity with Christ.

Right: Now is the time for Jesus to be glorified. In solidarity with Christ, we bring our praise.

All: The time is coming, Lord. With Christ, we must be buried and die, like a seed, so that we can become the fruit of your enduring love for the world. Amen!

LENT: WEEK 5B

A Zest for Joy and Praise

Exodus 17:1–7; Psalm 95; Romans 5:1–11; John 4:5–42

Left: We come with shouts of praise for Christ, who has restored a lasting relationship with our Maker.

Right: We bow down and honor our Creator, who makes us righteous by the loving sacrifice of Christ.

Left: We praise the Divine Spirit, whose presence bubbles up into eternal life for all who thirst for salvation.

Right: We sing of God's amazing grace and love for the whole world, for we know that Christ is reconciling all peoples of the earth—Samaritan and Jew, indigenous peoples and settler colonizers, _____.

Left: "God shows his love for us in that while we were still sinners, Christ died for us, in our hearts through the Holy Spirit, who has been given to us."[1] Such a relationship fills us with hope for praise.

Right: We kneel before our Lord and Maker, who has redeemed our twisted hearts and established a way of peace for us through Christ. We want to be disciples of Jesus forever.

Left: We pray for the Lord to remove the scales from those who fail to recognize the gift of Christ or who ask, "is the Lord really with us through these times of stress and war?" For we know that nothing compares to God's love for the whole world.

---

1. Rom 5:8.

Right: In desert times, we are prone to argue and complain. But we trust that trouble produces endurance in us, and endurance produces character, and the character of Christ in us produces hope.[2]

Left: We pray for Christ Jesus to quench our thirst his living water and to refresh our hearts with his grace and peace so that we can go out as harvesters, gathering fruit for eternal life from God's abundant fields.

Right: We sing praise to the Lord. We want to leap and roar for joy because God is the rock of our salvation.

All: We raise a joyful shout to Christ, who guards our hearts and souls and minds in love. Amen and amen.

---

2. Rom 5:3–4.

LENT—PALM SUNDAY: WEEK 6A

A Thank Offering of Joy

Isaiah 50:4–9(a); Psalm 118:1–2, 19–29;
Philippians 2:5–11; Luke 19: 28–40

All stand.

All: With unity of heart and voice, we join the great throng of faith to worship and praise you, Father, Son, and Spirit, with shouts of joy. Hosanna!

Women: Our worship is a heartfelt response to the wonderful gift of our Lord and Savior, Jesus Christ. Your grace has educated our tongues. Hosanna!

Men: God, you awaken our ear in the morning to listen for your voice.
Help us adopt the self-giving love of our Lord, Jesus Christ. Hosanna!

All sit.

All: The stone that the builders rejected has become the main foundation of the life of faith.[1]

Women: Hosanna in the highest!
Christ became like us, but entered our world as a servant of love, and his humble obedience led him to the cross.

---

1. Ps 118:22.

Prayers for the Season of Lent

Men: We praise Jesus, the name above all names.
We bow our knees and cry out, "Hosanna! Hosanna in the highest!"
As the father honors the name of Jesus, we, too, praise the Son—Jesus, the name above all names.

All stand.

All: Your faithful love, O Lord, lasts forever and ever.

Women: We reject all temptations to exploit the grace of Christ.

Men: Send us as cruciform servants into this weary, distressed, and war-torn world.

All: As a surging crowd, we rejoice in the peace of heaven and cry out, "Hosanna! Hosanna in the highest!"

LENT—PALM SUNDAY: WEEK 6B

Praise in a Hosanna Alphabet Key

Isaiah 50:4–9a; Psalm 118:1–2, 19–29;
Philemon 2:5–11; Matthew 21:1–11

Men	All praise to you, the self-giving Christ, our Lord, who loves the word and who stands before our neighbor.
Women	Because you humbled yourself, a festival of praise is ignited.
Men	Crowds continue to cheer, "Hosanna to the Son of David."[1]
Women	Disciples praise you by responding to your tasks and answering your call.
Men	Everyone is part of a chorus line to cheer, "blessings on the one who comes in the name of the Lord."[2]
Women	Forever is the timeframe of salvation, the time for a rich season of praise.
Men	Good God, we praise the name of Jesus, who in humility takes on our humanity.
Women	"Hosanna in the highest," the angels sing in harmony with the redeemed.[3]
Men	I will lift up your name on the streets of every neighborhood as a salvation celebration choir.

1. Matt 21:9.
2. Matt 21:9.
3. Matt 21:9.

Women	Jesus, you bear the glory of God to all—a light shining in the darkness.
Men	Knowledge of your presence with us in Christ is stunning, for your righteousness is a blessing to all generations forever!
Women	Let those who honor the Lord testify to his faithful love, which lasts forever and generates resounding praise.
Men	Many reject Christ, the cornerstone of salvation, and this astounds us.
Women	No one compares to Christ, who humbled himself to the point of death on a cross.
Men	Our honor is to Christ, and we surrender to his good future.
Women	People everywhere—in heaven, on earth, even under the earth—will bow and confess that Jesus Christ is Lord.
Men	Queues of the faithful form to sing, "Hosanna in the highest," to Jesus.
Women	Remember to open the gates of righteousness, Lord, so that our festival of thanks can pour into your presence.
Men	Shine your light on us as we go wherever you send us and do what you ask with joy.
Women	Thanksgiving and praise to Christ Jesus, for the day of God's love has come through you.
Men	Unless you build the house, Lord, it cannot stand, but with Christ as the cornerstone, you have built for eternity.
Women	Value for the earth, its coastlands and inhabitants, flows to all who wait in hope for you.
Men	Women, men, brothers, sisters, and friends who dwell in Christ—all humanity pays attention when you speak. Hosanna!
Women	eXpose your word to us, O Lord, and make your justice plain among the nations.
Men	Your salvation reaches all the way to the cross of Christ and the victory of his resurrection.

Lent—Palm Sunday: Week 6B

Women: Zion's daughters prepare to lead our preparations for praise.

All: "Hosanna, blessings on the one who comes in the name of the Lord."

LENT—MONDAY OF HOLY WEEK

Waiting with Praise

Isaiah 7:10–14; Psalm 40:5–10; Hebrews 10:4–10; Luke 1:26–38

People: O Lord, we declare your faithfulness for the world you made. We declare your salvation in Jesus. On the cross of Christ, we recognize your incomparable love. Your amazing trustworthiness looms before us.

Leader: We are waiting between sin, death, and the promise of resurrection. Instead of sacrifices and offerings, you prepare the body of your Son for all.

Left: After the dark night of sin and death, we wait with the comfort of your word, "do not be afraid."[1]

Right: After the dark night of sin and death, we wonder if nothing is impossible for you, Lord. Will your salvation truly come to us?

People: We confess to being a tiresome people. We have sinned against you and our neighbors, our sisters and brothers. Send your Son, "Emmanuel," afresh among us today.

Leader: As we wait for the righteousness of Christ to be revealed, help us listen for your still, small voice speaking among us.

Left: Holy Spirit, we trust that you are hovering over the darkness of our day. Your wonderful salvation wipes away the debt of sin. We give you praise.

---

1. Luke 1:30.

Lent—Monday of Holy Week

Right: Holy Spirit, we trust that you are hovering over the darkness of our day. Your amazing grace restores our sight and sets our feet on the path of life. We give you praise.

People: From our graveyard of sin, light is dawning on your plans for us.

Leader: As we wait for you to establish the reign of Jesus, your love is stirring in our hearts. In the long night, when we despair about sin, injustice, and evil in this world, fill our hearts with praise for your name that will echo throughout the whole world and the cosmos.

All: As we wait to be made holy by your will, we will praise your great and holy name together.

LENT—TUESDAY OF HOLY WEEK

A Living Sacrifice of Praise and Service

Isaiah 49:1-2; Psalm 36:5-11; Hebrews 9:11-15; John 12:1-10

Women: When we were powerless slaves to sin, without hope, you came among us as a liberator.

Men: When we felt we were doomed to be dead men walking, you laid a new covenant on the table and prepared a meal for us with Jesus.

All: Listen everyone, pay attention! You called your Son, Jesus, from the womb, and you are reaching out to the whole world through your Spirit. Your love overflows through us in a living sacrifice of praise and service in your name.

Women: Your loyal love extends to the skies and your faithfulness reaches the clouds. Your salvation extends to humanity and to all the animal kingdom. Your justice reaches the deepest fathoms of the sea.

Men: Your faithful love is as strong as the oldest mountains. The bounty of your house is an inviting feast, and your drink comes from the river of pure joy.

All: Listen everyone, stay attentive! We praise Jesus as the high priest of your new covenant law and amazing grace. Your love overflows through us in a living sacrifice of praise and service in your name.

Lent—Tuesday of Holy Week

Women: When the arrogant threatened to walk all over us and the threatening hands of the wicked began to choke our faith, you gave us refuge in the shadow of your wings.

Men: When our consciences were smeared with sin, you secured our deliverance for all time.

All: In the shadow of your wings, all of humanity can find refuge. We will sing of your love forever. Your beauty and fragrance fills the room. Your love overflows through us in a living sacrifice of praise and service in your name. Amen.

LENT—WEDNESDAY OF HOLY WEEK

Hearing, Seeing Praise

Isaiah 50:4–9a; Psalm 70; Hebrews 12:1–13; John 13:21–32

All sit.

Leader: The one who will declare our innocence is near. From the prison cell, the harsh wilderness, and the darkest of nights, our hearts are roused to praise.

Left: In the world, we encounter hard hearts and shameful behavior. We are in the wrestling grip of life and death.

All: Hurry into our tumult, Lord, deliver and help us now. *(Clap Clap).*

Right: In the world, we grow weary from the trials of famine, flood, and sickness.

All: Hurry into our tumult, Lord, deliver and help us now. *(Clap Clap).*

Left: The exploited earth is groaning. Pollution's aroma is sickening. The temperature is rising, and it is hard to breathe.

All: Hurry into our tumult, Lord, deliver and help us now. *(Clap Clap).*

Right: You have opened the ears of the poor and needy. We are listening for your voice.

All: Hurry into our tumult, Lord, deliver and help us now. *(Clap Clap).*

All stand.

Lent — Wednesday of Holy Week

Left: Without your love, our heads drop, and our hands are drained of life. Though you endured condemnation from sinners, you finished the race for the sake of the joy set before you.

All: We are ready to rejoice and be glad in your presence. *(Clap Clap).*

Right: Without your grace, we are in danger of giving up. But you endured the cross and ignored the shame of the jeering crowds.

All: We are ready to rejoice and be glad in your presence. *(Clap Clap).*

Left: Without your mercy, we struggle with the trappings of sin and become so easily distracted by money, sex, and power. But you didn't hide your face from sinners and outcasts. You accepted your cross-shaped calling and laid down your life for the sake of the world.

All: We are ready to rejoice and be glad in your presence. *(Clap Clap).*

Right: Lord, we long to hear your sweet voice declaring our innocence. Awaken us from our darkness to the good news of your saving help.

All: We are ready to rejoice and be glad in your presence. *(Clap Clap).*

LENT—THURSDAY OF HOLY WEEK

Dressed and Ready with Praise

Exodus 12:1–4a, 11–14; Psalm 116:1–2, 12–19;
1 Corinthians 11:23–36; John 13:1–17, 31b–35

Leader:	On the night Jesus was betrayed, he took bread and broke it. This bread is a symbol of his body, broken for us.
All:	We remember you with praise, Jesus. You are always tuned to our cries for help.
Younger: (<33 years)	We eat the bread until you return to broadcast your great love, for rich and poor alike.
	Help us be mindful of our selfish impediments to this witness as we eat with the joy of grace in our hearts.
Older: (>33 years)	We take the cup and remember your faithful salvation. You have reconciled us to one another through your sustaining, self-giving love.
All:	As we share this meal together, we are dressed and ready with praise, Jesus, even as you wash our feet.
Leader:	Jesus, our teacher and Lord, has shown us an example of self-giving love. He was broken to open the way for reconciliation. He is the great "I am" of the Father, who knows our name. He calls us into the refreshing joy of the Holy Spirit.
All:	We remember you with great joy, Jesus.

Lent — Thursday of Holy Week

Younger: We receive the new command to love each other with all your mojo. We surrender our tribal identities and seek fellowship with the diverse, intergenerational people of God.

Older: We have been trapped in the isolating grip of fear about the world around us and burdened by the fault line of sin within us. But your loving sacrifice on the cross catches us off guard, and so we embrace your command to love one another.

All: We remember you with great joy, Jesus.

Leader: Jesus, our servant, came as God among us with a towel around his waist. He calls us to serve our desperate world in the power of his resurrection humility.

All: We are dressed and ready for praise. We lift the cup of salvation and toast our servant King. We will praise your name for ever and ever. Amen.

LENT—GOOD FRIDAY: PRAYER A

Christ Between Us

*Isaiah 52:13—53:12; Psalm 22;
Hebrews 4:14-16, 5:7-9; John 18:1—19:42*

People: We are your people, gathered from the margins of sin.
Christ, you stand between us and a world that is bent away.

Leader: Who can believe what we have heard?
In our mind's eye, we see Christ exalted and lifted high.

People: But we saw you disfigured and were distressed by your demise.
Christ, you stand between us and a world that is bent away.

Leader: In God's plan, revealed upon the cross,
Christ stands between us and our rebellious, suffering hearts.

People: You are despised and avoided, tormented by both God and men.
Christ, you stand between us and a world that is bent away.

Leader: A lamb for the slaughter, pierced and crushed of life, the wounds of Christ bring us healing and make us whole.

People: We are a people, gathered at the margins of hope for salvation.

Lent — Good Friday: Prayer A

	Christ, you stand between us and a world that is bent away.
Leader:	From the cross, Christ cried out, *My God my God, why have you left me?*
	He drank the cup the Father gave him to its dregs and was poured out for all.
People:	We are a people, gathered at the margins of faith.
	Christ, you stand between us and a world that is bent away.
Leader:	Christ stands with all who are trapped in pride and doubt.
	Christ stands with us as we make our confession, raising us from struggle and sorrow.
People:	We are a people gathered from the margins of love.
	Christ, you stand between us and a world that is bent away.
Leader:	Christ is our great high priest, who has written a new covenant in our hearts.
	Jesus is the source of our salvation, whose grace compels us to love the broken and poor.
People:	Christ, you stand between us and your kingdom.
	You beckon us into the now and all that is yet to come through your love.

LENT—GOOD FRIDAY: PRAYER B

The Cross as a Signature of Love

Isaiah 52:13—53:12; Psalm 22; Hebrews 10:16-25; John 18:1-19, 42

Leader: From the groans and deep anguish of our world, we see the cross of Christ lifted high.

Right: As we look for the signposts of your self-giving love, we hear your cry from the cross, *My God, my God, you have left me alone.*

Left: You have been bruised and humiliated for our sins, pierced for our rebelliousness.

All: The deep anguish of the cross is your signature in love.

Leader: Lord, the whole world pants for your salvation.

Right: Lord, many are appalled to see your glory "dried up like a piece of broken pottery."[1]
Though you were crushed for our crimes, we remain blind and deaf to your love.
We acknowledge that we give you the blues.

Left: As we gather to gaze at your cross, place your word of love in our hearts and write your law of truth on our minds so that we will live in the world with your cross-shaped signature of love.

All: Pull back the veil so that all who seek you may find your grace.
May the good work of peacemaking end our terrible wars.

---

1. Ps 22:15.

Lent—Good Friday: Prayer B

May our discipleship be empowered by the Spirit to bring comfort on days of sorrow. Amen.

LENT—HOLY SATURDAY: PRAYER A

Waiting in Lament

Job 14:1–4; Psalm 31:1–4, 15–16; 1 Peter 4:1–8; Matthew 27:57–66

Our cry

Leader: Lord, we sit together in front of your tomb. Our hopes are dashed. Will your kingdom ever come?

People: Our hope in Jesus is laid in a tomb. Our faith is withering. Are you even listening?

Our complaint

Leader: The days of all who are born into the world are numbered. We are like flowers that bloom and then droop into the shadows. Our hope in Jesus feels like a trap. The gloating of our enemies is a torture. Have mercy. Hear our complaint, Lord.

People: We were ready to follow Jesus to the cross, but where is your deliverance? Have you brought us into a place of hope just to trick us? Have mercy. Hear our complaint, Lord.

Our request

Leader: Lord, you have promised never to let us be put to shame. We ache to see you coming quickly. We need you to lead us to peace for the sake of your name.

People: Please, Lord, shine your face on your people and gather us up in your faithful love. If Christ suffered for our human sin, set us free from the chains built by our desires. Our future is completely in your hands.

Lent—Holy Saturday: Prayer A

Our affirmation

Leader: We believe that salvation is in your bloodline, and so we praise you, trusting that your eyes are wide open to our plight.

People: We believe that in Jesus, a new day will come, and so we praise you, trusting that we can gather in the power of your love.

All: The dawn is breaking. We wait for you to turn our mourning into dancing.

Prayers for the Season of Easter

EASTER SUNDAY: WEEK 1A

Transcending Alarm: Living Celebration

*Isaiah 25:6–9; Psalm 118:1–2, 14–24;
1 Corinthians 15:1–11; Mark 16:1–8*

All: Who will remove our disgrace?
Who will wipe away the tears from our eyes?
Who will swallow the veil so that we can see God?
Who will take away the shroud of death?

Leader: Don't be alarmed!
God is good, and God's faithful love lasts forever.
God—Father, Son, and Spirit—is our saving help!

All: Why are there so many obstacles that imprison our hearts?
Why was God's cornerstone choice rejected?
Why was Jesus crucified?

Leader: Don't be alarmed!

Jesus of Nazareth, who was crucified, has been raised from the dead!

This is the day the Lord acted, the day the stone was rolled away!

Women: Christ died for our sins.
All: The Scriptures agree.
Men: Christ rose on the third day.
All: The Scriptures agree.
Women: I am what I am by God's grace.
All: The Scriptures agree.

Prayers for the Season of Easter

Men: On Mount Zion, the Lord will prepare for all people a rich feast of choice wines and select food, rich in flavor.

All: The Scriptures agree.

Leader: Don't be alarmed!

Jesus is alive! As he goes ahead of us into Galilee, let us follow him with songs of joy and deliverance.

Women: We confess that our lives are fractured, alienated, and unfulfilled.

All: The amazing grace of Jesus liberates us to sing joyful songs of salvation.

Men: As sinners, we confess that we consistently miss the mark of God's law and give him the blues.

All: The amazing grace of Jesus liberates us to sing joyful songs of salvation.

Women: Deliver us from violence in our homes. We especially pray for women who experience sexual violence and domestic violence. "How long, Lord?" we cry.

All: The amazing grace of Jesus empowers us to sing joyful songs of salvation.

Men: Deliver us from the evil of racism. We especially pray for the indigenous peoples of this world. In your eyes, Black lives do matter, Asian lives do matter, every life matters. We testify that love crosses every divide.

All: The amazing grace of Jesus unites us to sing joyful songs of salvation.

Leader: This Easter Sunday, we are not alarmed!

God has acted through the self-giving love of his son, Jesus, so that today we can shout for joy.

All: Alleluia!

Leader: God's grace is never for nothing. We will not be afraid, but will celebrate and worship God in the peace of Christ!

All: Alleluia!

EASTER SUNDAY: WEEK 1B

Who Rolled the Stone Away?

Isaiah 65:17–25; Psalm 118:1–2, 14–24; Acts 10:34–43; John 20:1–18

Leader: From the darkness of all death,
the light of the world bursts from the grave.
We bring our tear-drenched praise to the Father,
rejoicing that you have raised Jesus on the third day.

People: Praise the Lord! You have rolled the stone away, and today we hear the unexpected words of victory, *Peace be with you.*

Left: We didn't know who we were looking for until you called our names.

Right: When you called our names, we recognized you standing among us.

Left: In suffering and distress, we all were weeping,
looking in hope for your salvation.
Today we rejoice to see the risen one.

Right: Today we rejoice to stand with the risen one.
Though we face the suffering of war again,
we hold a new creation hope that all wars will cease.

Leader: We praise the impartiality of Father, Son, and Spirit.
We praise the God of creation and new creation.

People: We rejoice that the self-giving love of God becomes resurrection life for all who believe.

Left: Our sins blind us to who you are: the risen, conquering Son.
Bless us and our world with your peace.

Right:	Our sins wage a war within us.
	Today we run to you.
	Your name brings relief from our dark nights.
Left:	Thank you, Lord, for the cross and for resurrection peace.
	Continue to make us a delight.
Right:	Thank you, Lord, for the cross and for resurrection peace.
	May we live out of your attentive love and harmonizing presence.
Leader:	Today we rejoice that the Father has raised Jesus, his Son.
People:	Today we embrace the peace that the risen Jesus offers his people.
Left:	Today we praise the Spirit, who fills our hearts with love and promises to respond when we call on the name of Jesus.
Right:	Today the stone is rolled away.
	Jesus is risen, indeed!
Leader:	We have hope that wars will be no more,
	that suffering and distress will flee away,
	that the new creation will endure.
People:	Hallelujah! What a Savior!

EASTER: WEEK 2A

The Cross as a Signature of Praise

Isaiah 50:4–9(a); Psalm 31:9–16; Philippians 2:5–11; Matthew 26:14–27, 66

Leader: Praise Jesus, who chose not to exploit his equality with the Father and the Spirit, but emptied himself and came among us in human form as a servant.

People: Though we continue to betray you and one another, your self-giving love is new each day. As we take and eat your bread of life, may the cross become our signature of praise.

Leader: Praise God, who gives his word to greet us each morning. We celebrate our deliverance from sin, oppression and evil. Our future is in God's hands.

People: As disciples of your Son, we affirm our vulnerability.

Amidst the threats and grief of life, we need your face to shine on us.

Leader: Praise the spirit, who draws us into God's love.

People: If you helps u, who will condemn us?

Even when our vision fails, we trust that you will renew all things.

Leader: Christ invites us to take up the cup of wine, which has the signature of his blood, freely shed for the world in love.

People: We share this bread and wine in memory of your self-giving, servant love. We can accept any insult or offense through your signature of grace.

Leader: We praise Father, Son, and Spirit.
We bow our knees and confess that Jesus is Lord.

People: When life is consumed with groaning and persistent suffering, you empower us to give you praise. We take up your cross and follow you in joy.

Leader: This is our grateful commitment, our signature of praise.

People: Amen.

EASTER: WEEK 2B

Beautiful Things

Isaiah 55:1–11; Zephaniah 3:14–20; Psalm 16;
Romans 6:3–11; Luke 24:1–12

Leader:	Today, we focus our eyes on the cross of Christ.
All:	You call us to seek you here, because this is where you can be found.
Men:	Jesus, we listen for your word as we live. (*Clap clap.*)
Women:	We promise to abandon wicked schemes. (*Clap clap.*)
Men:	In resurrection power, you gather the outcasts. (*Clap clap.*)
Women:	You turn the shrouds of shame and guilt into praise. (*Clap clap.*)
Leader:	Beautiful things come from your hands. Your faithful loyalty never ends.
All:	During times of stress, you calm us with your love. When drum beats announce days of war, you calm us with your love. In times of climate grief, you calm us with your love. Amidst racial intolerance, you calm us with your love.
Men:	We have been baptized into your death, Jesus. (*Clap clap.*)
Women:	Free in your love, we are no longer slaves to sin. (*Clap clap.*)
Men:	You are risen from the dead, so we can walk in newness of life. (*Clap clap.*)

Prayers for the Season of Easter

Women: We came with fragrant spices, but rejoice to find your empty grave. *(Clap clap.)*

Leader: Today, risen Lord, we run to you with shouts of joy.

All: May your word be productive in our lives.
May we continue to do beautiful things by your hand.

Men: We bring grateful praise for the richest of feasts in the bread and wine.

Your faithful loyalty never ends, Father, for you have sent us your Son and the Spirit.

(Clap clap.)

Women: Jesus, you are our portion, our cup.
Spirit, you are our rest, the one at our right side. *(Clap clap.)*

All: Alleluia! Alleluia! Alleluia!
(Clap clap, clap clap, clap clap.)
Beautiful things! Beautiful things!

EASTER: WEEK 3A

A New Creation Prayer

Joshua 5:9–12; Psalm 32; 2 Corinthians 5:16–21; Luke 5:1–3, 11–32

All:	We gather to praise you, God, for your self-giving love in Christ, your Son, has swept us up as part of the new creation
Women:	The old has gone; the new has come.
	We praise you, our reconciling God, and are beside ourselves with wonder.
Men:	Lord, you watch our backs.
	Your faithful love surrounds us.
	We sing out for joy.
Leader:	We acknowledge that sin saps us like a summer drought and brings great pain to our lives, and so we confess our sin and ask you to surround us with songs of rescue.
All:	Our world is in the clutches of fear, war, sickness, homelessness, and despair.
	With the pressing crowds, we wait to hear your faithful words of comfort.
Women:	Christ, you roll away our disgrace.
	You heal our land and broken lives with your reconciling love.
Men:	We are your followers, Jesus, ambassadors of your reconciling love.
Leader:	Help us abide in your transforming love so that we can endure troubled times, for the sake of the world.

All: Father, Son, Spirit—
You are our secret hideout in danger.
You are our deserted place when we need refreshment.
May our new creation prayer become a resounding song of praise.

EASTER: WEEK 3B

Formed by God through the Faithfulness of Christ

Isaiah 43:16–21; Psalm 126; Philippians 3:4b–14; John 12:1–8

People sit.

People: We gather as a people formed in Christ, grateful that you have chosen us and aware that we are planting for a harvest in tears.

Leader: Lord, you are the host of this meal, and we need you to do a new thing among us.
We invite you to form us as your people through the faithfulness of Christ.
We ask you to send streams of your Spirit into our community.

People: As we sit down to eat with you, refresh us with your resurrection hope.
We are willing to leave the past behind and to reach towards your good future ahead. Your love is our best dream come true.

People stand.

Leader: In the power of Christ's resurrection and through your participation in his sufferings, may you know Christ and seek to be formed in his cruciform way.

People: We gather as a people formed in Christ.

Leader: With joyful shouts and gratitude, we eat this bread, broken for us, and drink this wine of Christ's redeeming love, shed for us.

All: Alleluia!

EASTER: WEEK 4A

Preservation Praise

Psalm 23; Acts 4:5–12; 1 John 3:16–24; John 10:11–18[1]

Leader: In these days of pandemic threat and fear, you are with us.

You protect our steps in the darkest of valleys.

You keep us alive to witness the power of your love.

Left: We are in need, and many who could help walk by.

Our conscience is perplexed by all the rules for isolation.

We cry out from the loneliness of self-distancing.

Right: We confess our fear in the common enemy who scatters us.

Our lives are threatened, and hope is a thin cord.

Hear our cry and gather us in your self-giving love.

Leader: Lord, we trust your goodness and faithfulness to protect and preserve us.

Your love is secure, because Jesus laid down his life for us.

Let him be our role model and captivate our imagination for self-giving love.

Left: Jesus, in these times of distress, remind us that you have conquered death and risen from the grave.

---

1. This prayer draws from NRSV.

Easter: Week 4A

Right: You alone can give us the confidence to love through these days that are darkened by threat and worry. By the power of your Holy Spirit, cause us to be people of kindness and praise amidst the shadows of death.

Leader: Grant us the strength and courage to cry out for our grief-stricken neighbors, those desperate for food and homes, those who are overwhelmed and turn to violence. In your love, hear our aching cry.

Left: God of vast love, we are all like sheep scattered in distress. Gather your flocks from the north, south, east, and west. As creation groans, bring your salvation near so that all can hear the voice of the good shepherd and worship you alone.

Right: In these days of fear, help us to love God and to love our neighbors as ourselves.

Leader: Though this pandemic threat encircles us, you have set a meal before us that is graced with truth and love. When the enemy of hard-hearted selfishness blinds us, you peel away the scales from our eyes by your self-giving love. When demons of loneliness, alcohol, and family violence threaten to tear us apart, you remain our cornerstone of salvation and hope.

All: You anoint us with the fresh oil of preservation praise. Alleluia!

EASTER: WEEK 4B

Creation and New Creation Praise

Psalm 148; Acts 11:1–18; Revelation 21:1–6; John 13:31–35[1]

Leader: Praise the Lord!
Over the seas, from the mountains, and through the valleys,
joy and delight return to you.
Today we join with creation's praise.

All: Praise the Lord!
We join as little children, running after Jesus.
May we love one another as you have loved us.

Leader: Praise the Lord!
You transform our sin-scarred lives and refocus our eyes so we can see the light of Christ shining over and out of everyone.
We join with the Holy Spirit in praising you for our new-life joy.

All: Praise the Lord!
We long for the day when all creation—the kings of the earth, young and old, male and female—will sing of your love forever.

Leader: Praise the Lord!
Our ears ring with the song of the new creation.
We anticipate the day when God will dwell with humankind, when every mourning wail will be transformed into praise.

1. This prayer draws from NRSV.

Easter: Week 4B

All: Praise the Lord!
We are being formed by the gospel, which is rich with hope.
Standing on our tiptoes, we yearn to glimpse the new heaven and new earth, where there will be no more mourning, crying, or pain.

Leader: Praise the Lord!
God of the new heavens and earth, your word is trustworthy and true.

All: Hallelujah!

EASTER: WEEK 5A

Local and Global Praise

Psalm 150; John 20:19–31; Acts 5:27–32; Revelation 1:4–8

Leader: Praise God, the self-giving Father, Son, and Spirit
Left: Let's get into praising God—Father, Son, and Spirit—like a jazz band, with all sorts of instruments improvising and joining in.
Right: Let every living thing—all creatures great and small—worship the Creator and Savior of the world.
All: Jesus, giver of peace, we welcome you with great joy.
Leader: When we encounter people and powers who push back against your gospel of grace, help us remain loyal and committed to you.
Left: We confess our human frailty and fear.
Right: We recognize the intrusive presence of the principalities and powers that influence our lives.
All: Breathe your Spirit upon us so that we might extend your reconciling love and forgiveness to the world.
Leader: Father God, lead us in your self-giving love.
Left: Holy Spirit, keep us courageous and faithful.
Right: Jesus, free us from our sin.
All: God of the universe, you are the Alpha and Omega. To you be glory and power for ever and always. Amen.

EASTER: WEEK 5B

Remaining in God's Love

Psalm 22:25–31; Acts 8:26–40; 1 John 4:7–21; John 15:1–8

Leader:	We gather to remember the Lord, who loves the world.
People:	Why are our leaders silent in the face of injustice?
	Why is there so little action in responding to our problems?
	We are worn down by racism, domestic violence, poverty, despair, and environmental distress.
Leader:	Christ, you cried out, *My God, my God, why have you left me all alone?*[2]
People:	If you molded us from clay, why are we now living as shattered pots?
	Why is our tongue stuck to the roof of our mouths?
Leader:	May all who are hungry and suffering eat of your goodness and be filled.
People:	Spirit, come afresh, and give us the cross-shaped humility of Christ. Move us into the sweetness of service, compassion, sharing, peacemaking, and bearing witness to your gospel of love.
Leader:	May we remember you as a lover, who first loved us.
	May we remain in your love as we seek to love the world and all it contains.
People:	We will remain in Christ, whose self-giving love remains in us.

2. Ps 22:1.

EASTER: WEEK 6A

Believing is Seeing

Psalm 30; Acts 9:1–6; Revelations 5:11–14; John 20:19–31

Leader: It's the first day of the week again.
People: We rejoice to see Jesus in resurrection power.
We rejoice that his light shines on us and this world.
People kneel
Leader: Jesus, you are the lamb of God, who was worthy to endure the cross.
People: Cruciform one, you are worthy of all glory, blessing, and honor.
We fall at your feet.
Leader: When we cry for help, you will lift us up.
People: Your healing frees us to sing your praises with all our sisters and brothers.
Leader: We grieve the darkness that threatens your peace—our sins, those who persecute your people, the principalities and powers of this world.
People: Yet your resurrection faithfulness turns our mourning into dancing.
Leader: We have come to gather at your table and to bear witness to your nail-scarred hands.
People stand
People: Breathe the Holy Spirit upon us and fill us with your resurrection peace.
Leader: In the fellowship of the Spirit, we see you, Jesus.

Easter: Week 6A

People:	In the sharing of bread and wine, we meet you, our Lord. *People arms outstretched*
Leader:	Lord, we humbly accept your calling to offer our hands in humble service of the world.
People:	May something like scales continue to fall from our eyes as we live out your gospel of grace.
Leader:	It's the first day of the week again. With believing hearts, we hear what we see in Jesus afresh.
People:	Refresh us, Lord, in this time of worship. Be with us when we go out in your name so that all may believe and see you.

EASTER: WEEK 6B

The Plain Truth

Psalm 23; Acts 1:36–43; Revelation 7:9–17; John 10:22–30

Leader:	We gather as a small part of the countless, multicultural people of God,
	who are listening for the voice of Jesus and seeking to follow his way.
All:	Praise to you, Lord Christ.
Right:	Jesus, you are our shelter.
	No one can snatch us from your hands.
All:	*(Shout)* Amen!
Left:	Father, Son and Spirit, you are the DNA of eternal life.
	We honor you.
All:	*(Shout)* Amen!
Right:	Jesus, your life, work, death, and resurrection reveal the plain truth:
	you are the Savior of the world, and so we give you thanks.
All:	*(Shout)* Amen!
Left:	Cruciform Lord, you will wipe away every tear of suffering.
	We bless your holy name.
All:	*(Shout)* Amen!
Right:	Servant King, you will satisfy our hunger and quench our thirst.
	In hardship and joy, you are our God forever and ever.

Easter: Week 6B

All:	*(Shout)* Amen!
Left:	Christ, you are the lamb who was slain on the cross, resurrected in peace, and exalted to your Father's throne. All wisdom, power, and might are yours.
All:	*(Shout)* Amen!
Right:	Jesus, you have led us to springs of life-giving water. You have transformed us to do good works.
All:	*(Shout)* Amen!
Left:	As we humbly recognize your self-giving love, we proclaim the plain truth:
	we want to fall face down and praise you day and night!
All:	*(Shout)* Amen! Amen! Amen!

EASTER—ASCENSION SUNDAY: WEEK 7A

Unstoppable Praise

Psalm 93; Acts 1:1–11; Ephesians 1:15–23; Luke 24: 44–53

Leader: We are compelled to bring unstoppable praise to Christ,
whom God established at the foundation of the world.

People: In Jesus, God's kingdom has come.
In Jesus, we are baptized in the Holy Spirit.

Leader: We are compelled to bring unstoppable praise to our risen Lord,
who gives us the gift of salvation.

People: In Jesus, God's kingdom has come.
In Jesus, we are baptized in the Holy Spirit.

Leader: We are compelled to bring unstoppable praise to Christ,
who suffered and rose from the dead on the third day.

People: In Jesus, God's kingdom has come.
In Jesus, we are baptized in the Holy Spirit.

Leader: We are compelled to bring unstoppable praise to Jesus, our ascended Lord,
who is seated at the right hand of God and whose powerful strength is our inheritance.

People: In Jesus, God's kingdom has come.
In Jesus, we are baptized in the Holy Spirit.

Leader: We are compelled to bring unstoppable praise to Jesus,
who fills us in every way and gathers us together as his unified body.

Easter—Ascension Sunday: Week 7A

People: In Jesus, God's kingdom has come.
In Jesus, we are baptized in the Holy Spirit.

Leader: We are compelled to bring unstoppable praise to Christ, whose unending song will echo to the ends of the earth forevermore.

EASTER—ASCENSION SUNDAY: WEEK 7B

Living Stone Praise

Psalm 31:1–5, 15–16; Acts 7:55–66; 1 Peter 2:2–10; John 14:1–14

Leader: Lord, you are the master builder, who fashions us as living stones in Christ Jesus.

Left: You established Jesus as the capstone of our praise.
We praise Jesus, our rock, who protects his living stones.

All: Hallelujah!

Right: Jesus, we recognize our tendency to reject your cross, and yet you continue to pull us from darkness into your redeeming light. You are the way, the truth, and the life.

All: Hallelujah!

Left: Lord, give us the faith to ask you for hope. We praise you for shining your face on us. Thank you that we can trust our future into your faithful hands.

All: Hallelujah!

Right: You are a rock who doesn't roll, and you will never let us be put to shame.

All: Hallelujah!

Left: We have tasted the goodness of God, your body, Christ, broken for us.

You are now the risen, conquering Son.

All: Hallelujah!

Easter—Ascension Sunday: Week 7B

Right: The Spirit keeps alive the story of your wonderful acts, Jesus, in glorifying your Father through your life, death, and resurrection. We take the wine in remembrance of you. In fellowship with you, we can know your Father.

All: Hallelujah!

Leader: We offer our lives as your "living stone" praise.

All: In your love, we become:

A chosen race,

A holy nation,

A people who are God's possession,

A royal priesthood.

We offer sacrifices to God in our praise, witness, cross-bearing lives, compassion, justice for the poor, and peacemaking. Hallelujah!

EASTER—PENTECOST SUNDAY: WEEK 8A

Pentecost Praise

Genesis 11:1–9; Psalm 104:24–36; Acts 2:1–21; John 14:8–17

Leader: Praise the Lord!
The great and glorious day of God has come to us.
In self-giving love, God comes to us as the Son.
In transforming power and joy, the Spirit is poured out on all.

Women: We rejoice to speak of our God.
Under the influence of the new wine of the Spirit, we prophecy.
We proclaim and testify that all who call on the name of Jesus will be saved.

Men: We praise in the power of the Spirit,
our advocate to bring us into the life of God.
We abide in the joy of this calling as the Spirit abides in us.

Leader: Our Pentecost praise is punctuated with celebration and joy.
Every rush of wind, every tongue of fire
reminds us of your presence as our comforter,
the one who guides us into all truth.

Men: We love you, Lord, and in the power of the Spirit,
we desire to follow Jesus,
to keep his commands, and to bless his holy name.

Women: We love you, Lord, and in the power of the Spirit,
we join with our brothers and sisters—young and old,
slave and free—to rejoice in your good work.

Easter—Pentecost Sunday: Week 8A

	May your glory endure forever!
Leader:	God of creation, we confess our failure to steward the earth.
	Continue to send forth your Spirit as an agent of creation amidst the loss of biodiversity that threatens our ecosystems.
Women:	God who loves the world as a mother,
	we confess our greed and great indifference as threats to your creation.
	Renew our world by the Spirit
	amidst the stains of pollution and the threat of climate change.
Men:	Like Babel of old, we confess our arrogance
	in living as if nothing we propose to do is impossible.
	Transform our hearts by your Spirit
	so that we will share the mission of your salvation in the world.
Leader:	Father, Son, Spirit, we recommit to your way of grace.
	As we share this bread and wine, sustain your memory in our hearts.
Men:	In this Pentecost hour, assure us of the truth of your saving word.
	In the fellowship of the Spirit, confirm us as the body of Christ.
Women:	In this Pentecost hour, restore us to our calling to creation care.
	May our lives be the new wine of the kingdom in the world.
All:	In this Pentecost hour, we follow Jesus into the world
	to speak the language of your great love.
	In this Pentecost hour, abide in us as we abide in you.
	Hallelujah!

EASTER—PENTECOST SUNDAY: WEEK 8B

Pentecost Doxology

Ezekiel 27:1–14; Psalm 104:24–34, 35(b); Acts 2:1–21; John 15:26–27, 16:4(b)–15

Men: Lord, we proclaim our doxology of praise.

You are our Father, and you send the Son and Spirit into the world.

You are the Son in glory at the Father's right hand.

You are the Spirit sent from the Father to testify for the Son and lead us to truth.

Women: Lord, we join the doxology of praise.

You are the Father who plans your love for the world.

You are the Son who incarnates Triune love.

You are the Spirit who guides us into the Father's plans in gentleness or a fierce wind.

All: In Jesus your righteousness is revealed.

In his death, your face is hidden.

In his resurrection, we catch a vision of eternity.

We will sing our praise for as long as we can.

Women: We praise God—Father, Son, and Spirit—who has done countless good things.

And yet we cry out bitterly, for our days are filled with the dry bones of war, and the shrieks of the injured are in our ears.

Easter—Pentecost Sunday: Week 8B

Men: Father and Son, send the Spirit to companion our leaders toward peace.

Your Spirit alone can empower the soldiers, generals, and business tycoons of war to beat all swords into ploughshares.

All: Lord, we gather to bless your name.

Hear our cries for peace.

Send your comforting Spirit to all who are overwhelmed and broken by brutal conflict.

Men: Lord, by your Spirit, we live in true hope and joy.

Send your regenerating Spirit to calm the groaning despair of all who are waiting on you, especially those in war zones.

Women: Lord, you are open-handed and generous.

Send food and refreshing rains into the war zones.

All: Lord, we call upon your saving presence.

Rise up as the Prince of Peace.

Shake up all cabinets of war with the power of your love.

Send your Spirit as a gentle dove to receive our doxology of Pentecost praise.

Prayers for the Season of Ordinary Time

ORDINARY TIME—TRINITY SUNDAY: WEEK 1A

Praise to the Father, Son, and Spirit

Proverbs 8:1–4, 22–31; Psalm 8; Romans 5:1–5; John 16:12–15

All stand.

All: In salvation's freedom of frolicking delight,
we praise the living God,
whom we know as Father, Son, and Spirit.
We worship the Creator, self-giving lover of all.

Left: Father, Son, and Spirit, your name and reputation is majestic.
Your glory is on display in your handiwork—all star fields, grass plains, seabeds.
We proclaim you as the Lord of Lords.

Right: Our praise draws us into the inviting relationship of the Trinity.
Out of your mutual sharing, you pour your love into our hearts.
Your fingers have formed us to be just a little below the angels.

Left: With joy we acknowledge the wisdom of your relational creativity.
The smile of your beauty in the creation welcomes us into each day.
The skill of workers mirrors your handiwork.
The joy of living comes from your breath, O God.

Prayers for the Season of Ordinary Time

Right: Father God, we are amazed at your salvation!
Because we are sinners, we can gratefully recognize the self-giving gift of your Son. You dismantle all our self-seeking ways.
We have been redeemed by the faithfulness of Jesus and the faith you have given us.

All: Hallelujah! We praise the Father, who pours his love into our hearts.
We praise the grace and truth of Jesus.
We praise the Spirit, who helps us to see Jesus in our midst.

Left: Living Jesus, you usher the hope of God's glory into our lives.
You bring the peace of God to all who call on your name.

Right: Holy Spirit, you are a gift that keeps on giving.
Through our trouble, you develop endurance within us.
In endurance, you mold our character in Christ.
Formed in the character of Christ, you secure our hope in God.

All: Father, the universe declares your glory and majesty.
Jesus, in you we see the love of your Father.
Spirit, we are open to your guidance.
We are all ears for the fresh word you want to speak to us.
Lead us into the truth of becoming sons and daughters of God. Amen.

ORDINARY TIME—TRINITY SUNDAY: WEEK 1B

Embracing Thankfulness

*Genesis 1:1–2:4a; Psalm 8; 2 Corinthians 13:11–13;
Matthew 28:16–20*

Leader:	We gather in the name of the Father, Son, and Holy Spirit.
All:	All thanks to the God of love and peace, eternal embrace of Father, Son, and Spirit, who draws us into the life-giving relationship of the Trinity.
Right:	Bless this day of creative goodness. We greet the handiwork of your fingers in the skyline of sun, moon, and stars.
All:	Thanks be to God!
Left:	God of surprises and restful delight, we welcome your invitation to steward the glory and grandeur of your creation.
All:	Thanks be to God!
People:	Our morning thanks arises from your purposeful, creative Spirit moving in our lives. Our evening thanks recognizes your presence through the day.
All:	Praise be to you for the encouragement and grace of your embrace.
Leader:	Lord, every step we take is on your holy ground. Though you crown us with glory and grandeur, keep us humble in heart. With songs of thankfulness, we respond to your call to care for your creation.

Prayers for the Season of Ordinary Time

All: Thanks be to God!

Right: As brothers and sisters, we willingly receive this bread in remembrance of your deep love in Christ. We are truly grateful. By your Spirit, we commit to live in harmony with each other.

All: Thanks be to God!

Left: May the fellowship of the Spirit be with us. With gratitude, we receive the wine in remembrance of the saving, world-changing death of your Son. Dear Jesus, come near and speak with us in this meal.

All: Thanks be to God!

People: Our morning thanks arises from your purposeful, creative Spirit moving in our lives. Our evening thanks recognizes your presence through the day.

Praise be to you for the encouragement and grace of your embrace.

All: In the name of the Father, Son, and Holy Spirit, thanks be to God!

ORDINARY TIME: WEEK 2A

Let . . . so that . . .

Psalm 67; John 14:23–29; Acts 16:9–15; Revelation 21:10, 22–25

Left: *Let God* grant us grace and blessing,
make his face of love to shine on us,
and bless us through the gifts of creation.

Right: *So that* your way, God, is known to us
and your salvation is declared to every tribe, language, and nation—
to the far ends of the earth.

All: *Let the people* thank you with mind, body, and heart,
celebrate you with shouts and joy,
and bring you the gift of overflowing love.

Leader: *So that* your justice shines bright throughout the universe,
and your wisdom is declared to the world as a trustworthy guide.

Left: *Let God* love his people and
speak his word.

Right: *So that* we will love God
and keep his word.

All: *Let the people* praise God, who shows us his love through his son, Jesus.

Leader: *So that* we will remain in Jesus, God's word of love,
and enjoy God's companionship in the Spirit.

Left: *Let God* in greatness receive the resurrected Christ.

Prayers for the Season of Ordinary Time

Right: *So that* we will flourish in the peace that Jesus leaves with us.

All: *Let the people* abide in the fellowship of Father, Son, and Spirit.

Leader: *So that* we can go into the world
to proclaim the good news of the new creation
through our lives.

Left: *Let God* be the new creation's light through Jesus
and establish your holy city as a foretaste of the kingdom that is to come.

Right: *So that* The nations will walk toward eternity in the light,
and your people will worship you alone.

All: *Let the people* trust your promise, visions, and dreams
with the now—but not yet—eyes of faith,
which perceive that the gate to your good future is never shut.

Leader: *So that* our names will be registered in the Book of Life,
and we will witness the rulers of the earth
bringing their glory to the city of God.

All: Amen.

ORDINARY TIME: WEEK 2B

Resolved to Serve God with Joy

Psalm 47; Acts 1:1–11; Ephesians 1:15–23; Luke 24:44–52

People: We rise to join in joyous praise to God.

Leader: Our God—Father, Son, Spirit—is King over the nations.

People: In this time of climate crisis, we acknowledge that we are the earth's guardians, and the leaders of our nations belong to God.

Leader: Christ, who washes our feet, is the head of the church

People: God has placed everything under the feet of Jesus, who gives us the Holy Spirit, who has the power to release us from fear, strengthen our faith, and energize our love for our neighbors.

Leader: From the north, south, east, and west, we applaud your self-giving love in Jesus, and we cry for mercy for our world. Remember to do good for your people.

People: We clap our hands with joy as we recognize the gift of your self-giving love, which flows daily over your people. Sustain us, protect us, and give us peace so that this love will spread throughout the world by the power of your Holy Spirit.

Leader: In this time of fear and uncertainty, ignite our imagination for how we can serve you by the power of the Spirit.

People: Your grace has changed our hearts and forgiven our sins. Transform our lives by the way of the cross and the power of the resurrected Christ so that we can become the hands and feet of Jesus as we hear the cries of distress, mental anguish, and brokenness around us.

Leader: Incarnate, crucified, and resurrected Lord, we declare that our hope is in you alone.
May your grace and truth remain with us and embrace our world, today and evermore.

People: May your wisdom illuminate the world so that all will know that you are good.
Amen. We shout for Joy!

ORDINARY TIME: WEEK 3A

Praise for God's Faithfulness

1 Samuel 8; Psalm 138; 2 Corinthians 4:13–5:1; Mark 3:20–35

People:	We thank you, God, with all our heart. You have made the name of Jesus greater than anything. May your kingdom come. May your will be done in our lives, communities, and your world.
Left:	On the day we cried out, you answered us. You encouraged us with your unseen presence and gave us inner strength.
Right:	Whenever we are in deep trouble, you make us live again. Your spirit provides us with an enduring, welcome home. This is our unseen, real hope.
Left:	In our world, many have abandoned your rule. Some say, "Jesus is out of his mind."[1] Others accuse, "Jesus has an evil spirit."[2]
Right:	Father, Son, and Spirit, we confess that you are our King. You have "bound the strong man" and delivered us from evil.[3] You will continue to save us with your strong hand.

---

1. Mark 3:21.
2. Mark 3:30.
3. Mark 3:27.

Prayers for the Season of Ordinary Time

People: We recognize our failures as your people. We have pursued our own power and influence over others rather than following your will. We have promoted our interests ahead of the way of your Son. We have fallen for the temptation to worship the false gods of money, national prosperity, regional prestige, comfort, and power.

Left: Strengthen our faith when we face scrutiny and rejection. Give us eyes to see your grace working throughout our world.

Right: We commit to the way of the cross, knowing that your power will raise us up with Christ.

Left: We pray that your hope for the new creation will become evident in our community. May the gospel prosper. May those who are broken-hearted be healed. Lift up the poor, the victims of loneliness and despair, those who are overwhelmed by domestic violence. Break the chains of racial, gender, and childhood injustice in our world. Hear the cries of your people for relief. Be with the families of all who are living in fear. Save those who are caught in the power of alcohol and drugs. Bring all people the peace of mind and heart that comes through your Spirit.

Right: We earnestly pray for your lasting faithfulness. Together we cry out, "do not let go of what your hands have made."[4] May your kindness be revealed so that the rulers of the earth will give you thanks. Multiply your grace so that the gratitude of your people will bring you glory.

People: Lord, hear our prayers. May the life of Jesus, in the power of the Spirit, fill our lives. Send us as brothers and sisters of Christ into the world so that we can live as transparent witnesses of his love for all. Amen.

---

4. Ps 138:8b.

ORDINARY TIME: WEEK 3B

Praise Chant

Deuteronomy 30:1–10; Psalm 100;
1 Corinthians 3:10–17; John 15:1–8

Men: What do we want, God's people? What do we want today?

All: We want to sing and make music to you among the nations. We want to praise Jesus' name in the power of the Spirit. *(Clap clap.)*

Women: What do we want, God's people? What do we want today?

All: We want to remain in Jesus and live productive lives of grace. We want your kingdom to come so that we can sing of your glory all over the earth.

Children: What do we want, God's people? What do we want today?

All: We want our hearts to give you unwavering praise for your faithful love. We want to sing and shout with praise that awakens the dawn. *(Clap clap.)*

Men: What do we want, God's people? What do we want today?

All: We want to be led into your sanctuary of peace. We want to celebrate your salvation, which makes us fully alive. We are changed by Jesus and want to give you praise. *(Clap clap.)*

Women:	What do we want, God's people? What do we want today?
All:	We want to obey your voice with our whole heart, being, and mind so that we can be set free serve you. We want to step back into line with our praise. *(Clap clap.)*
Children:	What do we want, God's people? What do we want today?
All:	We want Jesus to be our only foundation. We want you to nourish us so that our lives will produce the fruits of grace and burst forth with praise for the exalted name of Jesus.
Men:	What do we want, God's people? What do we want today? Hey!
All:	Today we want to give God holy praise. Hey!
Women:	What do we want, God's people? What do we want today? Hey!
All:	Today we want to praise God for his steadfast love, compassion, and forgiveness. Hey!
Children:	What do we want, God's people? What do we want today? Hey!
All:	Today, we want to be reoriented by grace so that we can offer pleasing praise to the Father, Son, and Spirit. Amen! *(Clap clap.)* Hey!

ORDINARY TIME: WEEK 4A

A Discipleship Lament

*2 Kings 2:1–2, 6–14; Psalm 77:1–2, 11–20;
Galatians 5:1, 13–15; Luke 9:51–62*

All: We are your disciples, Jesus, but the road to the cross is hard to follow. Many refuse to welcome us in your name. We are crying out loud, and our spirits are growing weary as we wander through this desert without any comfort.

Women: When we face trouble, help us look for you. Hear our prayer, Lord, and don't hesitate, for we are being consumed by frustration and despair.

All: Your freedom is precarious, Lord. Sometimes we are looking down the barrel of slavery again. We are a selfish people, and we so often turn away from you and turn on each other. In our frustration, we want to call on your "fire from heaven" to consume our enemies.[1]

Men: As we walk this hard road of following you, pressure is building, excuses are flying, and our complaints are wearing us out. We can no longer see your footprints in the sand. We no longer feel certain that you are with us.

All: Lord, we need you to reveal your strength to us again. Show us how you can pass through a wild desert storm and cross over raging seas. Bring a windstorm from heaven to lead us to freedom once again.

---

1. Luke 9:54–55.

Women: Restore our confidence that you will come to our aid when we face trouble, Lord. We need the gift of your presence so that we can respond to one another with love instead of resentment and anger. Help us remember the joy of our salvation so that we will be listening for your voice and will hear you when you call us to follow you out of our comfort zones.

All: We are comforted as we remember the story of your liberation in our lives, how you have nourished the life of the church and rescued your people throughout history. You have performed wondrous and surprising acts of grace in the world. We believe that your kingdom is drawing near, and so we give praise to your great and holy name.

Men: As we look for you in kindness and mercy, you meet us as we are. As brothers and sisters in Christ, we want to love our neighbor as ourselves.

All: We can stand firm as we follow our Lord, for the rhythm of each step is becoming a song of joy and praise. Hallelujah!

ORDINARY TIME: WEEK 4B

New Creation Praise

2 Kings 5:1–14; Psalm 30; Galatians 6:7–16;
Luke 10:1–11, 16–20; 1 Corinthians 11:23–26

All: Praise the Lord! *(Clap.)*
Our experience with the dark night of weeping confronts us,
counterbalancing the joy that is new each morning.
In Christ, we proclaim that your new creation is everything!

Leader: Lord, our prayer gathers the love you have put into our hearts.
We pray in the memory of Jesus, who, on the night he was betrayed, took the bread.
Make us one as we share this meal.

All: Praise the Lord! *(Clap.)*
We will not be silent.
Though your anger over our sin lasts for a moment, your love lasts for a lifetime.[1]

Leader: Lord, you send us ahead into the world on the mission of your kingdom, but you promise to join us.[2]
At this table, you join us for your meal on the way.
You sit among us and give thanks as you break the bread, reminding us of your favor.

---

1. Ps 30:5.
2. Luke 10:1.

Prayers for the Season of Ordinary Time

	You feed us with your grace, which we celebrate again today.
All:	Praise the Lord! *(Clap.)*
	We gather as your body.
	Nourished by your love, we are prepared to serve you as we go out into the world.
	You turn our sadness, struggles, and pessimism into dancing.
	You clothe us with joy.
	We long to fulfill your law by bearing one another's burdens.
Leader:	Lord, we accept times of testing as opportunities to strengthen our faith and enliven our praise for you.
	As we eat your bread and drink your cup, we proclaim the liberating death of Christ until he comes in glory!
	May the whole world recognize you as we do.
All:	Praise the Lord! *(Clap.)* We travel light.
	Praise the Lord! *(Clap.)* We reap eternal life.
	Praise the Lord! *(Clap.)* We are crucified with Christ.
	Praise the Lord! *(Clap.)* We go into the world with words of peace.
Leader:	Today, Lord, we proclaim together in Christ,
	New creation is everything!
All:	Praise the Lord! *(Clap.)*
	(Shout) Amen!

ORDINARY TIME: WEEK 5A

Enduring Despair and Embracing Joy through Praise

Amos 7:7–17; Psalm 82; Colossians 1:1–14; Luke 10:1–10, 16–20

People: We inhabit the freedom of praise for the Father, Son, and Spirit. You have gifted us with the inheritance of light. In days of despair, we can endure through the patient presence of the Spirit. In days of joy, the fruit of the Spirit grows into the praise of delight.

Leader: We praise you, Lord of heaven and earth. Your kingdom has come to us in the unexpected grace of Christ Jesus. All our yearnings are fulfilled by your self-giving love, which we joyfully receive through your Spirit. All praise to your name.

People: We acknowledge that we don't measure up to your plumb line, for we fail to give justice to the lowly and orphan and to maintain the rights of the poor and destitute.

Leader: Our hearts cry out, "how long, Lord? . . . how long?"[1] Listen to the desperate weeping in _____ and _____. See the desolation in _____ and _____. Rescue the lowly and needy from the power of the wicked. Send us into these places of oppression as servants of your grace.

---

1. Ps 82:2.

People: We are ordinary people, Lord, but we surrender to your will, and we are ready to speak, act, and love wherever there is despair. Through our faith in Christ Jesus, we thank you for the outworking of love among and through your body of Christ. We wait together for despair to be captured by joy so that all the people of the earth will join your creation in declaring your praise.

Leader: We are ready to receive your commission. The ends of the earth wait for the presence of your kingdom. Help us to live worthy and fruitful lives that are and empowered by the Spirit and pleasing to the Lord so that we can give you praise through our good works and deepening knowledge of God.

All: As people rescued from darkness and despair by Christ Jesus and adopted into your love, we ask you to send us into the world as laborers, prepared to reap a harvest of love and joy beyond all we can imagine. Hallelujah!

ORDINARY TIME: WEEK 5B

Praise to the Name of Jesus

Amos 8:1–12; Psalm 52; Colossians 1:15–28; Luke 10:38–42[2]

Leader:	We gather to remember and praise God for the mystery of "Christ in us, the hope of glory."[3]
Men:	We confess that we are often tempted to boast, create mischief, and love evil more than good. In the midst of this world, your name is truly good.
Women:	We confess that our tongues can be razor sharp, that we often smother the truth with lies, and that our words devour the poor in our land. In the midst of this world, your name is truly good.
Men:	We confess that we snatch at false riches, which tear us away from your comforting presence. Our sins threaten to uproot your steadfast love in our lives.
Women:	We confess that we sometimes embark on a desperate search for personal happiness. We contradict your grace through our expectations of others. We are worried and distracted by many things. Forgive us, Lord, and welcome us back to sit at your feet.

---

2. All readings for this prayer draw from NRSV.
3. Col 1:27.

Prayers for the Season of Ordinary Time

Men: We praise the name of Jesus,
the image of the invisible God,
the firstborn of creation,
the one who holds all things together.
Glory be to God, the Father of our Lord Jesus Christ.

Women: We join in praising the name of Jesus,
the first born of the dead,
the head of the church,
the bearer of hope to all creation.
Come, Holy Spirit, come!

Leader: Reconciling God—Father, Son, and Spirit—
our deep desire is to praise you with the energy that Jesus inspires within us.

All: Our praise arises from the conviction of this mystery:
"Christ in us, the hope of glory." Hallelujah!

ORDINARY TIME: WEEK 6A

Backs to the Wall Praise

1 Samuel 17:57—18:5, 10-16; Psalm 9:9-20;
2 Corinthians 6:1-13; Mark 4:35-41

People: We come in awe to praise your name, Lord, for there is none like you. You are the one who brings us back from the edge when our life hangs in the balance.

Left: We come to rejoice in your salvation. We dug a hole for ourselves when we strayed from following Jesus and sought to micromanage our own lives.

Right: We are overwhelmed when your enemies sin against us and want to see us suffer. We have been through disasters, stressful situations, and times of great pain. Yet even on our sleepless nights, we rise to praise your enduring love.

Leader: When our backs are to the wall, your grace covers us. When we feel like we are dying in body, heart, and mind, you give us your peace. We open our hearts and seek to praise you with thanksgiving.

People: We come in awe to praise your name, Lord, for your word can calm any storm. Your love is without limits.

Left: Thank you for being with us in the boat as we drift through the storms of life. In your guiding hands, the gospel of love will reach the whole world. Every tongue, tribe, and nation will declare your praise.

Prayers for the Season of Ordinary Time

Right: When you call us to minister across divides, we confess our fears. We are afraid of abuse and failure, rejection, and contempt. Root our confidence in Christ alone.

Leader: When our backs are to the wall, your grace covers our backs. When it feels like we are dying in our body, heart, and mind, you give us your peace. We open our hearts and seek to praise you with thanksgiving.

People: We come in awe to praise your name, Lord, for you empower us to serve the broken and needy. We commend the broken in heart, mind, and body to your healing.

Left: Through Jesus, you establish patience, purity, knowledge, and generosity in our lives. You offer your salvation to those who are unknown as well as well-known, poor and rich, false and real, victim and abuser. All can gratefully sing of your amazing grace.

Right: You put Christ's love in our hearts and you fill us with the graced power of the Holy Spirit. In times of hunger or plenty, imprisonment or freedom, hard work or abundant providence, you remain with all who seek you.

Leader: You, Lord, are a safe refuge for the oppressed and for all who are living through difficult times. Father, Son, and Spirit, hear the cries of all who are suffering and crying out for help. You are the God of justice and salvation. We stand together in your peace to shout out and sing your praise.

All: Amen, amen.

ORDINARY TIME: WEEK 6B

Lament in the Cause of Mercy

2 Samuel 1:1, 17–27; Psalm 130;
2 Corinthians 8:7–15; Mark 5:21–45[1]

Women:	There is always death in the battle for victory, the struggle for power. We are overwhelmed by the blood of the slain, the pale faces of those who were loved and cherished.
Leader:	Look and see, Lord. With fear and trembling, we tell the whole truth.
Men:	The lands of Gaza and Ashkelon are soaked in misery and despair, swarming with suffering, without hope. We cry from the depths, Lord, asking for your mercy and justice to flow into these contested regions like a mighty, rushing stream.
Leader:	Lord, hear our cry. With fear and trembling, we tell the whole truth.
Women:	Have you turned your back on the evil that is raging in these war zones? Have you turned your face away from the desperate and displaced? Have you withdrawn the gifts of your grace and mercy in our time?
Leader:	Lord, are you listening? With fear and trembling, we tell the whole truth.

---

1. All readings for this prayer draw from NRSV.

Men:	When will the madness of war end? When will your mighty hand save again? The earth is scorched. The world you created in love is groaning. The people you made in your image are suffering. Has darkness overwhelmed your providence? Where is your redeeming hand?
Leader:	Lord, hear our complaint. With fear and trembling, we tell the whole truth.
Women:	Lord, we recognize that if you kept track of our sins, none of us could stand before you. We need your forgiveness and grace to fall over us and our enemies like a soaking rain after a long drought. We need you to assure us that neither life nor death can separate us from your love.[2]
Leader:	Lord, hear our confession. With fear and trembling, we tell the whole truth.
Men:	Lord, you call us to do justice and to love mercy. We are waiting with our whole being for you to act with justice and to show mercy to your hurting world. In Jesus, you became poor for our sake. Your strong and faithful love has the power to make all wars cease, to destroy the weapons of war, and to restore peace to all the people of the earth.[3]
Leader:	Lord, hear our prayer. With fear and trembling, we tell the whole truth.
Women:	Lord, we trust in your mercy. When we reach out to touch you, you will heal us. When you hear the groaning of creation, you will pour your healing over the land. When we praise you in faith, you will save your people and send us out in peace.
Leader:	Lord, this is our lament in the cause of mercy. Hear our prayer.

---

2. Rom 8:39.
3. 2 Sam 1:27.

Ordinary Time: Week 6B

Men: Christ Jesus, we trust that you have broken the power of death. You have suffered to redeem us and wipe away our tears. Your grace flows over all enmity, conflict, and hatred. You alone are to be praised!

Leader: Lord, this is our lament in the cause of mercy. Hear our prayer.

ORDINARY TIME: WEEK 7A

Together in Lament

Genesis 22:1–14; Psalm 13; Romans 6:11–23; Matthew 10:40–42[1]

Leader: How long, O Lord? Will you forget us forever?[2]

People: We have waited patiently, and we are longing to worship as your gathered people. We are ready to receive the sweet fellowship of the Spirit among us.

Leader: Lord, we remember your provision to Abraham. You have provided the Lamb who was slain, the one who pays the wages of our sin.

People: We trust your unfailing love to remain close to us in times when we feel isolated and alone. Our hearts rejoice in your salvation, the gift of Jesus, our Lord.

Leader: How long, O Lord, must we wrestle with our thoughts? Every day we have sorrow in our hearts.

People: We cry out for our world, which is gripped in distress. Have mercy on our neighbors near and far. Comfort us as we suffer the loss of hopes, dreams, work, and life.

Leader: Lord, we remember your goodness. We rejoice that you chose to enter into our world through the life and death of your Son, Jesus.

People: You have sent us into the world as people of the gospel. We want to sing of your love forever.

---

1. All readings for this prayer draw from NRSV.
2. Ps 13:1.

Ordinary Time: Week 7A

Leader: Look on us, God of steadfast love. Remember to bring light to the eyes of your people so that we will see you and your way in our troubled world.

People: We thank you for remaining with us in this time of trial. We are the daughters and sons of Abraham, and we trust your blessing to bring us home rejoicing.

All: Today we count ourselves "dead to sin but alive to you in Christ Jesus."[3] Through your grace, make us instruments of righteousness and justice in our homes, neighborhoods, and throughout the world. We praise you, Father, Son, and Spirit, forever!

---

3. Rom 6:11.

ORDINARY TIME: WEEK 7B

Praise for God's Restoring Gaze

Genesis 22:1–14; Psalm 13; Romans 6:12–23; Matthew 10:40–42

Leader: Lord, you are a gift-giving God. In Christ Jesus, you bless us with eternal life. Today, most merciful one, accept our heartfelt praise.

Women: Left to our own wits, we could never come into your presence. Yet your love compels us to surrender to you. Through Christ you beckon us into the sweet spot of justice and righteousness.

Men: Alone, we confess that agony fills our hearts. We recognize how easily our bodies can be weaponized for sin. We confess that without your amazing grace through Christ, we readily follow the whims of sin.

All: Lord, look with love upon us. Restore sight to our eyes so that we can sing of your salvation, proclaiming your goodness for all.

Women: We trust in your faithful love. The gospel of Jesus has transformed our lives. Thank you for all who have ministered your grace to us.

Men: We give thanks for your healing power, which is active within us and throughout your world. Thank you for setting us free from our slavery to sin. Look upon us in grace and empower us in the Spirit as ambassadors for your mission in the world.

Ordinary Time: Week 7B

All: Gracious and merciful God, accept our heartfelt praise. We commit to follow Jesus all the days of our renewed lives.

Women: You call us to gather and to share a meal in your presence. Your body has been broken to set us free from sin. This is the bread of life, which brings rich fellowship to your people through the Spirit.

Men: We rejoice that sin no longer holds power over us. In your restoring gaze, we see the blazing light of love, for you surrendered your Son on the cross for our redemption. In obedient remembrance, we drink the cup.

All: Jesus, together we offer you a song of praise. You were sent to us from the Father and obedient to the costly love of the cross. We give you thanks.

Leader: Your people are united in praise! God, our Father, thank you for the enduring gaze of your love toward the world through Jesus, your son.

All: Hallelujah. Amen.

ORDINARY TIME: WEEK 8A

Praise for Our Forever and Always God

2 Samuel 5:1–5, 9–10; Psalm 48; 2 Corinthians 12:2–10; Mark 6:1–13

Leader:	All praise to you, father, Son, and Spirit. You are our God, forever and always.
	You will lead us faithfully to the very end of our days.
People:	Through your healing and liberating power, the lame leap for joy and the blind see.
Men:	In success and failure, sorrow and happiness, you are our God forever and always.
Women:	From birth to the end of our days, in sickness, times of testing, and good health,
	you are our God, forever and always.
Leader:	In seasons of growth and decline, you reveal yourself as our refuge. For the self-giving love you showed us through the cross of Christ, your praise extends to the far corners of the earth.
People:	We confess our tendency to be unfaithful. We have failed to love our neighbors. We have traded insults with our enemies. We have put aside righteousness and resisted your justice. Forgive us for our sins, which quench your enlivening spirit, and wash us clean with your liberating grace.

Ordinary Time: Week 8A

Men: Our dignity is secure in your faithful love. By the grace of Jesus, we can accept vulnerability and insults, and we can endure disasters, harassments, and all kinds of stress. Though we are living through difficult days, we affirm that you are our God, forever and always.

Women: We reject all forms of coercion and domination, for we want to be ruled by Christ's power alone. We affirm that when we are vulnerable for Christ, we become strong in the power of the resurrection. As we follow you into the ways of peace and the self-giving love of Jesus, we affirm that you are our God, forever and always.

Leader: To all who have ears to hear, we declare to our community and our world the surprise of your commitment to save and heal through your self-giving love. You created and continue to sustain the beauty of our earth. We give you thanks for your never-ending love and mercy.

People: Father, Son, and Spirit, refresh us in these days of stress. Keep us in the safe fellowship of the Spirit. Gather us together as one body in Christ. Heal our sick, comfort our broken-hearted, and renew the joy of those who are despondent.

All: You are our God, forever and always.
You are the one who will lead us faithfully to the very end of our days. Amen.

ORDINARY TIME: WEEK 8B

Coming into God's Presence

*Genesis 24:34–67; Psalm 43:10–17;
Romans 7:15–25a; Matthew 11:10–19, 25–30*

Leader: Lord, in your wisdom, you came into our world through the humility of the cross. Our hope is in you alone.

People: We come into your presence mourning the tragedy befalling our world. In our time of distress, we cry out, *Does hope come in a leaky bucket?*

Leader: Lord, in your wisdom, you made the crucified Christ the Lord over all creation.

People: Through the life-giving resurrection power of Jesus, we want to follow Christ into the crises of our world. We want to enter our homes, workplaces, and neighborhoods as servants of the crucified Jesus.

Leader: Lord, in your wisdom, you established Christ as the head of your church and call us to live in love, just as you and your Son live in love.

People: Protect us from greed, pride, and vainglory. Transform our lives so that we can become agents of your hospitality in the world, friends to tax collectors and sinners.

Leader: Lord, in your wisdom, you created your people in joy and established them to sing and delight in your love.

People: Through the power of your cross-shaped love, fill us with compassion, healing, and service so that your name will become the talk of the town.

Ordinary Time: Week 8B

All: Lord, we come as those weary and heavy laden.
We ask for your grace to assure us that we are "set free from the law of sin and death."[1]
We ask for your grace to do your will in the new normal of our lives.
We ask for your grace to help us see new missional possibilities in our neighborhoods.
We acknowledge your grace in giving us the gift of Christ so that we can be at home with you forever.
Amen.

---

1. Rom 7:24–25.

ORDINARY TIME: WEEK 9A

Kingdom of Heaven Praise

Genesis 29:15–28; Psalm 128; Romans 8:26–39; Matthew 13:31–33, 44–52

Leader: Kingdom of heaven praise is not a competition for the stars. God has shown great initiative in sending us the wonderful gift of his Son. He remembers our sin-soaked distress, and he removes our shame. Hallelujah!

People: Kingdom of heaven praise honors our master, who delights in perseverance, diligence, and hard work. In times of weakness, God's Spirit gives voice to our heartfelt praise.

Leader: Kingdom of heaven praise is like a court scene, where Christ pleads our case, and God chooses to acquit rather than convict us. For Christ died and was raised up to empower us so that we could offer kingdom of heaven praise.

People: Kingdom of heaven praise is a family of sisters and brothers of Jesus, God's Son. Together, we are being conformed to the image of Christ, God's righteous and holy one.

Leader: Kingdom of heaven praise is like a jeweler, searching for valuable pearls, who discovers that God did not spare his own Son, but gave him up to save us all. When we surrender our lives to the amazing grace of Jesus, we praise his name forevermore.

Ordinary Time: Week 9A

People: Kingdom of heaven praise is like a treasure hidden in a field, and when we walk in God's ways, the days of our life will be marked by goodness and God's great love.

Leader: Kingdom of heaven praise plants the smallest of seeds, which then bursts into life and becomes a stout tree that shades all who seek rest beneath its branches.

People: Kingdom of heaven praise is like the yeast worked into dough. God gives us the gift of his daily bread of love through Jesus our Lord.

Leader: Kingdom of heaven praise is like a net cast into the sea, which is so full of fish that we can barely haul it to shore. With joy, we complete our mission in Jesus' name.

People: Kingdom of God praise is like a teacher who brings together the fullness of God's word, testifying that God works all things together for good. Indeed, God is a lover who calls his people to sing glory and praise without ceasing.

All: Kingdom of Heaven brings his people peace so that we can faithfully praise his name, forever and ever. Amen and amen.

ORDINARY TIME: WEEK 9B

Lament in Times of Trouble

Hosea 1:2–10; Psalm 85; Colossians 2:6–15 Luke 11:1–13

All:	Lord, these are difficult times to worship you with joy. Will you be mad at us forever?
Women:	We faithfully desire to remain attached to your love and compassion.
	Yet we feel as if you are saying to us, "you are not my people."[2]
	With the whole world, we battle against fear.
	Alone, breathless, and weak, we are losing our vision for hope.
Men:	Lord, won't you bring us back to life again?
	We ask for your healing for the earth, but the heat and drought intensify.
	We ask for daily bread, but our appetite fails.
	We are crying out for better circumstances, pleading with the resurrected Christ to be victorious over the dark powers of these days.
All:	The whole earth is groaning with the threats of climate change, financial scams, and war. Why is your anger prolonged?
	Your silence is unnerving.
Women:	Lord, forgive all our wrongdoing.
Men:	Lord, cancel out our debts.

2. Hos 1:9.

Ordinary Time: Week 9B

All:	Lord, hear our prayers for your people and the world you love in Christ.
Women:	Father, lead us not into temptation through our despair.
Men:	Deliver us from chaos and evil.
All:	In this time of climate change, we cry out for you to be kind to your land, to expose fraudsters, and to make wars cease.
	Show us your faithful love and restore the joy of our salvation.
Women:	Lord, refresh us with your Spirit.
	Return to your gift-giving ways.
	Anchor our lives in Christ.
	Build up our faith so that we will overflow with thanksgiving to you.
Men:	Lord, without your fresh grace, we are slaves to our own wisdom, obliged to human tradition and the way the world thinks and acts.
	Set us free through your self-giving love in the cross of Christ.
All:	Lord, by the light of Christ, help us to recognize your disciples as those bringing food to the hungry and unemployed.
Women:	Lord, by the light of Christ, help us to recognize your disciples as those supporting strangers and visiting the lonely.
Men:	Lord, by the light of Christ, help us to recognize your wisdom in all who are seeking to understand, prevent, and manage this climate crisis for the common good. We echo our prayer for those working to prevent fraud and to bring wars to cease.
All:	Lord, as disciples of Jesus, we gather to pray, share, care, advocate, and worship together in the light of Christ. Break the power of fear and death so that the whole world can come to life in Jesus, our Savior. Father, may your kingdom come!

ORDINARY TIME: WEEK 10A

What the Redeemed Say

Hosea 11:1–11; Psalm 107:1–9, 43; Colossians 3:1–11; Luke 12:13–21

All: From the north, south, east and west, we join the global praise of your people.
Your goodness comes to all, without racial, cultural, gender, or class distinction.
With joy, we proclaim that Christ is in all things and with all people.

Left: Lord, we admit that our lives are bent on turning away from you and falling prey to sexual immorality, moral corruption, lust, evil desires, and greed.
Hear our penitent cries and re-establish your love towards us.

Right: Like strong-willed children, we seek to break free from your nurturing love.
We let anger, rage, malice, slander, obscene language, and lying have free range in our lives and in the church.
Hear our penitent cries and re-establish your love towards us.

All: We are redeemed people, humble recipients of the self-giving love of God.
With Christ, we die to sin, and through the power of the Spirit, we are raised to new life in Christ. Hallelujah!

Left: Lord, we recognize that we have wandered into the wilderness and lost our way.
We have been hungry and thirsty for your love.

Ordinary Time: Week 10A

Right: We admit that we have let the chains of greed and the seductive power of fame and prestige tangle our feet.

All: But we cried out to you in the dark of night, and you heard us and comforted us with your goodness.
Though we slipped and fell, your strong arm reached out to pick us up.
You unbound us with your self-giving love and delivered us from our slavery to sin.

Left: Liberating God, spread the table of your faithful love before us.
Feed us with the bread of life so that we can be one as you and Christ Jesus are one.

Right: Redeemer God, thank you for the costly love of Jesus, which is poured out for all as the wine of your new covenant.

All: Father, Son, and Spirit, we praise you for showing us how to walk in grace.
Thank you for your protection during times of loneliness, fear, sickness, and chaos.
Lord, we know you as the God who heals, protects the weak, and comforts the sorrowing.
We are your people, and we proclaim that your faithful redeeming love last forever!

ORDINARY TIME: WEEK 10B

Grace Expanding Praise

2 Samuel 11:1–15; Psalm 14; Ephesians 3:14–21; John 6:1–21

All: Our hearts contract and groan with the evil all around us, but today we rejoice because your grace covers our sin. We are all masters of betrayal and deceit, but we rejoice in the salvation of Jesus and celebrate God's faithfulness in joy.

Women: From previous generations and those yet to be born, we pray for your transforming grace to visit every human frame and to give us all—both sinners and saints—hope on our most lonely days.

Children: We are ready to learn about your love—how wide and long and high and deep it is. We want to catch where love flows, so we can praise and thank you from head to toe.

Men: Glory to Christ, who sits with our world. He sizes up our hunger, gives thanks, and breaks all the bread we need. Nothing is wasted by Christ Jesus, our King.

All: You are watching for the wise and those who seek you. You are eager to provide refuge to the faithful and salvation to those who love you. Glory to your name.

Women: When we were afraid, you offered us peace and set our feet on dry land. You give us strength, and your Spirit fills us with the rich gifts of grace.

Ordinary Time: Week 10B

Children: Ground us with the strong roots of your love and include us in your embrace.

Men: We seek the fullness of God so that we can be free from sin and shame. In Christ, we are your righteous ones. Our praise is bold and fills out our lives through grace upon grace.

All: When darkness comes, protect us from despair. Revive us when storms abound. Take the little we have and let your grace for the common good flow. We want to praise you until the end with grace expanding praise.

ORDINARY TIME: WEEK 11A

Prayer for Light in Times of Darkness

Genesis 32:22–31; Psalm 17:1–7, 15;
Romans 9:1–5; Matthew 14:13–21

Leader: Our Father, we call out, "tilt your ears towards us now. Listen to our prayer."[1]

People: We need you to save us in these days of climate crisis. Hear the cries of your creation for help. Make us vessels of care and instruments of your love.

Leader: Red, yellow, black, and white—we are *all* precious in your sight. In Jesus, you are putting the world right. Look upon us and see the help we need.

People: Like Jacob, we are wrestling through a dark night. Father, Son, and Spirit, comfort us and prepare us for the future so that we can live as your reconciling people and emissaries of your grace for the whole world.

Leader: Lord, show us the light of your love in our troubled times. Help us stand in solidarity with those who are suffering in our world.

People: Jesus, hear the cries for mercy from those who are sick and fill us with your compassion. We pray for our neighbors globally and locally in _____.

---

[1] Ps 17:6.

Ordinary Time: Week 11A

Leader: Jesus told his disciples, "you give them something to eat,"[2] and so we pray for the Spirit to fire our imaginations for how we can help all who face food insecurity. Bless our loaves and fishes.

People: Father, you have always been a refuge for your children. With your strong hands of love, protect the weak and vulnerable at this time. May the self-giving love and resurrection of Christ be our anchor in this storm.

All: We bless you, Father, Son, and Spirit, for our inheritance in your new creation. Cause our hearts to burn with love for all our neighbors. Fill us with the vision of your glory in your Son, who rules over all things. Together in Christ, we bless your name forever.

---

2. Luke 9:13.

ORDINARY TIME: WEEK 11B

Lament in the Spirit

Genesis 32:22–31; Psalm 17:1–7, 15;
Romans 9:1–5; Matthew 13:1–9, 18–23

Our Cry

All: Lord, we are troubled as we pass through this dark night. We are struggling with your call on our lives, and we are wrestling with selfish, indulgent choices and our secret thoughts that despise and judge others.

Women: Our minds are unsettled. We know that so many need housing, financial relief, refuge from violence, and protection from online bullying.

Men: Our hearts are exhausted by the evil that confronts our world at every turn. Wars rage. Our restless night seems unending. Hear the cries from your suffering world.

Leader: We are wrestling to see signs of your love as we ache for our convulsing world. But we will persist until you give us your blessing.

Our Complaint

All: In the darkness, we strain to see your face. When will you tilt your ears and hear our cry?

Women: Lord, violence has many faces. We are peering for glimpses of your refuge, of your strong hands that can save us.

Ordinary Time: Week 11B

Men: Lord, the violence of our world divides and traumatizes us. Show us where there is shallow water so that we can cross over into safety. Lead us to those who are speaking your truth in love.

Leader: Lord, come to us in the dark night of our perplexity and despair. Lead us in hope to the breaking of your dawn.

Our Request

All: Awaken us from our dark night, Lord, so that we can see your face and be saved.

Women: Read our lips, Lord. We desire to be productive in the power of the gospel. Release us from our limp faith so we can rejoice in the Spirit.

Men: Check us over closely, Lord. You have tested us through the night and have examined our hearts. We want to grow out of the good soil of faith. We are listening closely for the word you are speaking to us. We want to praise you, Jesus, as our Lord and God.

Leader: God, our Father, you have set our feet on your path of self-giving love. We call on you to manifest your faithful love in our lives and throughout the world.

Our Affirmation

All: Spirit, hear our cries, complaints, and requests. Receive them as an offering of praise and bring us together as one in fellowship to remember and be grateful for all you are doing through Jesus, our Lord.

Women: Lord, we know you are full of mercy. Through the unexpected power of the cross, we know you are saving the world. We praise you, Father, and with our brothers and sisters, we share this bread, broken for us, in remembrance of Jesus.

Men: Father, we know of your gracious love in Jesus. We gather with our sisters and brothers to drink the wine, the blood of the new covenant. Through the power of the Spirit, we celebrate your coming kingdom.

Leader: Jesus, as adopted children, we are planted in the good soil of grace. You invite us to come to you with our cries, complaints, and requests. As we lament in the Spirit, we discover a full voice for praise.

All: May all glory, blessing, and honor be to you—Father, Son, and Spirit—forever and ever. Amen.

ORDINARY TIME: WEEK 12A

Embracing the Fullness of Christ

*2 Samuel 11:26—12:13a; Psalm 51:1–12;
Ephesians 4:1–16; John 6:24–35*

All: We offer praise to the one true God—Father, Son, and Spirit.
As God's people, we acknowledge our purpose to serve and build up the body of Christ.

Women: Our calling is to reflect the unity of the Trinity and the love of Jesus, God's son.

Men: We seek to grow into the fullness of Christ.

Leader: We are one body, and we are one in Spirit. God calls all his people to one hope, the cruciform, resurrection life of Christ. We praise you, Lord Jesus.

All: We affirm our commitment to accept each other with kindness and to speak the truth with love. We can live in this way because you first loved us.

Women: In the world, it is easy to be tossed and blown by the stormy winds of financial stress, loneliness, fear, climate chaos, and more.

Men: You desire us to live in truth, to avoid doing evil in the Lord's eyes, and to act with compassion in the world.

Leader: We confess our sins against our neighbors. We have failed to be faithful stewards of your creation. We have sinned against you, O Lord, in thought, word, and

Prayers for the Season of Ordinary Time

	deed—by what we have done and by what we have left undone.
All:	Our father, we long to hear the promise, "I have removed your sin from you."[1]
	Wash us and we will be whiter than snow.[2] Wipe away our guilty tears.
	Thank you for appointing Jesus as your agent for life.
Women:	In your great mercy, you will not throw us out or remove your Holy Spirit from us.
Men:	We long to hear joy and celebration once again.
	Sustain within us a willing spirit that trusts and obeys.
Leader:	All who come to Jesus, the bread of life, will never be hungry.
	God sent Jesus to feed and give life to the whole world.
All:	For the life of the world—
	Jesus proclaims good news to the poor;
	Jesus delivers the joy of salvation;
	Jesus is victorious over evil;
	Jesus draws together his church in unity and peace;
	Jesus invites us to grow in his likeness;
	Jesus calls us to be good stewards the earth.
	Amen! Amen! *(Clap clap.)*

---

1. 2 Sam 12:13.
2. Ps 51:7.

ORDINARY TIME: WEEK 12B

Praise of a Homecoming People

Isaiah 1:1, 10–20; Psalm 50:1–8, 22–23;
Luke 12:32–40; Hebrews 11:1–3, 8–16

Leader: Father, Son, and Spirit, you speak to us through the cosmos from sunrise to sunset.
You come day and night to speak to your creation.
Receive our praise as you come among us today.

People: As your little flock, we bring a sacrifice of thanksgiving.
We come as a bride for Christ, our groom.
Receive our joy as you come among us today.

Left: You delight to give your kingdom to your people.
Yet you have come among us as one dressed to serve, a servant full of a groom's joy.

Right Even though the whole creation carries the sound of your voice,
we are amazed to encounter your self-giving love in this meal that you prepared for us today.

Leader: Lord, we hear your voice at the borderland of our waiting and are ready to open the door when you knock today.

People: You are the source of our faith, the fullness of our hope.
But we confess that we sit at your table, marked by the stains of sin.

Prayers for the Season of Ordinary Time

Left: We accept that you close your eyes to our outstretched arms of praise
when we fail to do good by not defending the orphan
or standing up for the displaced children of the stolen generations.

Right: We accept that you close your ears to our prayers when we fail to stand in solidarity with the oppressed in our community,
or when we turn away from the pleas of widows and families broken by violence.

Leader: Lord, even as you monitor the world for justice and righteousness,
you are always ready to settle the score on our sin.
But even when our sins are as scarlet,
you make us as white as snow through the grace of Jesus.

People: Thank you for serving us the bread of life, the body of Christ, broken for us.
Thank you for serving us the choicest of wines, the blood of Christ, shed for our redemption.

Left: Like Abraham, we want to step out in faith.
In fullness, we go out from our shared meal as a homecoming people,
looking for the dwelling place of your faithful people.

Right: Merciful God, without you, we would be strangers and immigrants in the world.
But you have redeemed us, and with grateful faith, we share the fellowship of joy today.

All: Amen. *(Clapping.)*

ORDINARY TIME: WEEK 13A

Prayer for Faith with Loving Action

Proverbs 22:1–2, 8–9, 22–23; Psalm 125; James 2; Mark 7:24–37

Leader:	The peace of the Lord be with you.
All:	May peace be on all God's people.
Women:	We surrender to God's strong hand of love and trust that this bond will last forever.
Men:	We surrender to God's strong hand of love and trust his protection will last for all eternity.
Leader:	We live in the world with those who believe that God is weak and unfaithful.
All:	May God demonstrate his strength and faithfulness to all people.
Women:	Forgive us when we deny your faithfulness by not taking cross-shaped action in our lives.
Men:	Forgive us when we deny your faithfulness by showing favoritism toward rich and important people and dishonoring the poor and weak on the margins of our community.
Leader:	Scripture teaches us, "As the lifeless body is dead, so faith without actions is dead."[1]
All:	We are genuine, fair dinkum when we confess our desire to love our neighbor as ourselves.

---

1. Jas 2:26.

Prayers for the Season of Ordinary Time

Women:	Lord, bless the prophets of our time and protect them when evil calls our for their heads on a platter. Bless the poor and suffering in our world.
Men:	Lord, bless all who are seeking to spread the good news of your coming kingdom throughout the world. Surround them with your strong shield and defend them.
Leader:	We love you Lord Jesus. Fill us with the living water of your truth so that we are known for love in action.
All:	God, you are the only hope for our confused and chaotic world. We cry out in distress from all the political chaos, war, natural disasters, and mental and social confusion. We ask you to remove the rod of wickedness from among us.[2]
Women:	We cry out for your salvation and peace in this world. May your mercy overrule judgement.
Men:	We cry out for your peace upon the people of God. We plead, "Lord do good for people who are good."[3]
Leader:	Jesus, you bring in a kingdom of peace and reconciliation. In a world of hurt, may we be your agents of peace.
All:	Father, Son, and Holy Spirit, we ask you to breathe your peace into our lives and actions. Amen.

2. Ps 125:3.
3. Ps 125:6.

ORDINARY TIME: WEEK 13B

Planet-Shaking Hope

Jeremiah 1:4–10; Psalm 71:1–6; Hebrews 12:18–29; Luke 12:49–56

Leader:	Praise God—Father, Son, and Spirit—who bends toward us and hears our cries for salvation and help.
Children:	Hey God, you knew us before we were born. You made our bellybuttons. Thank you!
Adults:	Lord, our lives are in your hands. We take refuge in you and give you our unshakeable praise.
Leader:	Praise God, who gathers us as his children. Though our world is filled with complacency, evil, and hard-heartedness, the Father draws near to us.
Children:	We love you and we want to do what you say, Jesus.
Adults:	Lord, we recognize the harm that our sin and evil do to our world. We wait for you to come as a burning fire into our darkness, to dance in our shadows, to arrive as a whirlwind or trumpet blast.
Leader:	Praise God, our rock and refuge, who saves us in love and protects us from the wicked.
Children:	We trust you and want to grow up in Jesus. We want to join the angels around you and dance in a festival of joy.
Adults:	Lord, we are not afraid of your judgement, for you have our backs, and you won't let us be put to shame. Hallelujah!
Leader:	Praise God, who floods the whole world with grace and mercy.

Prayers for the Season of Ordinary Time

Children: Please rescue our crumbling world and keep us safe so that we can shake, rattle, and roll with the joy of being your friend.

Adults: Lord, you alone are our planet-shaking hope.

All: Your kingdom cannot be shaken. We give you thanks and praise. Lead us out to serve your planet with care and love. Amen.

ORDINARY TIME: WEEK 14A

Rejoicing Together

Jeremiah 2:4–13; Psalm 81:1, 10–16;
Hebrews 13:1–8, 15–16; Luke 4:1, 7–14

People: Rejoice and shout to God—Father, Son, and Spirit—who is the lover of all. Your love is like that of a delighted groom.

Leader: God says, *I love my bride, the church.*
I want to fill you with good things.
All who hunger for life and love, open wide.
I provide loving spoonfuls of the Spirit out of covenant love!

People: We rejoice and say, *we love you Lord!*
Our lips carry the fruit of our joyful praise.

Leader: God says, *I love my bride, the church.*
Trust me, and I will be your strength.
Avoid the love of money and don't test me.

People: We rejoice when you delight in us, and your love gushes in our hearts.
We are filled with your Spirit so that we can love one another, welcome all, and share what we have with others.

Leader: God says, *I love my bride, the church.*
I will listen tenderly to you.
I will adorn you with assurance, help, and protection from your enemies.
I will cultivate you with my love so that you will be like a well-watered garden.

People: We confess there are times when our willful hearts have led us into the wilderness.
We have stopped listening to your voice and followed our own ways.

Leader: God says, *I love my bride, the church.*
I will redeem my people and restore my bride. I will you embrace you as family.
I will lead you out of the wilderness on my arm.

People: We rejoice in loving you, Jesus, our crucified and resurrected groom.
Thank you for delivering us from slavery and sin.
Thank you for empowering us for service by your spirit.

All: You, our loving and loyal Lord, beckon us to come and be filled with honey from the rock.[1] You lead us to life everlasting! Amen.

---

1. Ps 81:16.

ORDINARY TIME: WEEK 14B

Praise for the Name of Jesus

1 Kings 8:22–30, 41–43; Psalm 84; Ephesians 6:10–20; John 6:51–58

All:	Father, Son, and Spirit, we spread our hands toward the sky. As your living temple, we gather to bring a sacrifice of praise to the holy name of Jesus.
Women:	Heaven cannot contain you, Lord. Though the earth is distressed, you hear our cries for help. You bring salvation in Jesus' gracious name.
Men:	Living God, you are the bread who redeems our life. Your self-giving love is poured out like wine. Our yearning hearts are filled in Jesus' blessed name.
Women:	Lord, how lovely is your dwelling place. Wildlife and all creation sing a song of thanksgiving in Jesus' precious name.
Men:	Lord, we celebrate your kingdom joy, where immigrants and seekers all delight in the justice proclaimed by sweet Jesus' name.
Women:	Strengthened and protected by Christ alone, through days both dark and good, we trust you to defeat all evil in Jesus' compassionate name.
Men:	All rulers, authorities, and cosmic forces are hidden in the mystery of Christ, the Lord.

Prayers for the Season of Ordinary Time

	So we rise up with cheers and shouts to praise the glorious name of Jesus.
All:	Father, Son, and Spirit, we spread our hands toward the sky.
	As your living temple, we gather to bring a sacrifice of praise to the holy name of Jesus.

ORDINARY TIME: WEEK 15A

Praise from the Bottom Up

Genesis 3:1–15; Psalm 105:1–6, 23–26, 45b;
Romans 12:9–21; Matthew 16:21–28

All stand.

All: Our lives are lost in the love of Jesus. In him, we have found real life. Hallelujah!

Left: Though we often go with the flow of temptation and fail to discern good from evil, you are holy and make your righteous deeds known to all. All praise to you, Creator God!

Left sit.

Right: You call us to bless, not curse, and to stand with those who are happy as well as sad. Clothe us with Jesus so that we can seek to defeat evil with good.

Right sit. Women stand.

Women: We praise the Lord with joy in our hearts, for you sent your son, Jesus, to suffer, be crucified, and rise again on the third day to save us and the whole world. Hallelujah!

All stand.

All: Our praise comes from the bottom up. Your people can live as one body in Christ.

Right sit.

Prayers for the Season of Ordinary Time

Left: We come together to share the bread of heaven, Christ's body broken for us. We are compelled by love to share this beautiful feast. Hallelujah!

Left sit. Right stand.

Right: We come together to share the wine of heaven, Christ's blood poured out to give us salvation and dignity. Hallelujah!

Right sit. Men stand.

Men: We praise the Lord with joy in our hearts, ready to deny ourselves, take up the cross, and follow Jesus. We surrender all to you, our true life, for the hope of glory.

Men sit. Left stand.

Left: Father, Son, and Spirit, we lift our voices in harmony with your word. We cry out for your "marvelous works and justice to be declared."[1]

Left sit. Right stand.

Right: We commit to love our neighbors without pretending and to "defeat evil with good."[2]

All stand and join hands.

All: As we enter into your welcome, may our bottom-up praise be infused with the fire of your Spirit, and may we faithfully serve you and the world as your kingdom comes. Hallelujah! *(Clap clap clap.)*

---

1. Ps 105:5.
2. Rom 12:21b.

ORDINARY TIME: WEEK 15B

Refreshed in the Love of Christ

Jeremiah 18:1–11; Psalm 139:1–6, 13–18;
Luke 14:25–33; Philemon 1:1–21

Leader:	Praise the Lord, who draws us together.
All:	We gather to receive God's wonderful word and to be refreshed in the love of Christ. We gather as wayfarers to share his meal, the bread and wine of the presence of Jesus.
Leader:	Praise the Lord, whose welcome is wide.
All:	We gather as unique individuals to offer a unified song of praise. We gather aware of your gaze. We gather to be enfolded by your love. We gather to be held in the wisdom of your gaze, trusting your plans to inform our lives.
Leader:	Praise the Lord, who knows us through and through.
All:	We gather with all our flaws, knowing we have not always done the right thing. We have clung to family and our own life goals rather than following your cruciform path. We gather to surrender to your self-giving way of love.
Leader:	Praise the Lord, who forgives us when we confess our sins and turn to Christ.

Prayers for the Season of Ordinary Time

All: We gather as dearly loved co-laborers in Christ, inviting you to
build and plant in our lives and in your body, the church.
We gather as clay vessels, ready to be remolded by your creative hands so that grace and peace will flourish in our lives.

Leader: Praise the Lord, who refreshes us in the love of Christ.

All: We gather as sisters and brothers in the self-giving love of Christ.
We gather with thanks for each other and our world.
We gather to celebrate this foretaste of your consummating presence in the new creation.

All stand.

Leader: Praise the Lord, who makes war to cease, who holds back catastrophes and disasters
and heals our lives and lands in peace.

All: *(Shout)* Praise the Lord!

ORDINARY TIME: WEEK 16A

Wholehearted Praise

*Song of Songs 2:9–13; Psalm 45:1–2, 6–9;
James 1:17–27; Mark 7:1–8, 14–15, 21–23*

Left: We rejoice to sing praises to our loving God, who has spoken to us in Christ.

Right: We love to shout, "the season of singing has arrived."[3]

Leader: We rejoice in the freedom of your grace, and we seek to praise you with our whole lives, in both word and deed.

Left: We desire to *walk* the *talk*, Lord. May our work for justice and peace be a pleasing aroma to you.

Right: We desire to *walk* the *talk*, Lord. When we see the poor and outcast in the dust, stop our feet so we don't walk on by. Help us to raise them up to honor your name.

Leader: We rejoice in the freedom of your grace, and so we seek to praise you with our whole lives, in both word and deed.

Left: Your marvelous word has stirred our hearts. We welcome your truth, grace, and humility so that we might pour it into the world.

Right: Your marvelous word has stirred our hearts. We praise you, Creator of starfields, sun and moon, the earth and all it contains.

---

3. Song 2:12.

Prayers for the Season of Ordinary Time

Leader: We rejoice in the freedom of your grace, and so we seek to praise you with our whole lives, in both word and deed.

Left: You have anointed us with the oil of joy and given us new birth. We humble ourselves and offer our lives as a living sacrifice in the service of your creation.

Right: You have anointed us with the oil of joy and given us new life. We ask you to help us be quick to listen and slow to speak, quick to love and slow to anger.

Leader: We rejoice in the freedom of your grace, and so we seek to praise you with our whole lives, in both word and deed.

Left: We welcome the gospel you have planted within our hearts so that we can joyfully care for orphans and widows in distress and love our neighbors as we love you, Lord.

Right: We welcome the gospel you have planted within our hearts so that we can let go of worldly desires and hand-me-down rules and shout out your name with joy.

Leader: We rejoice in the light of your freedom and grace, and so we seek to praise you seek to praise you with our whole lives, in both word and deed.

Left: Jesus said, "It's from the inside, from the human heart, that evil thoughts come."[4] So we embrace your call to restraint and ask you to turn our hearts from theft, deceit, sexual sin, and every evil action, trusting that you, Jesus, bear our shame.

Right: Jesus said, "It's from the inside, from the human heart, that evil thoughts come." So we embrace your grace and ask you to turn our hearts from foolishness, arrogance, greed, envy, and an insulting tongue, trusting that you, Jesus, lift our burdens at Calvary.

All: Through Christ, we are your instruments for praise. Our hearts join together as one to give you praise for Jesus. The time for wholehearted praise has come!

---

4. Mark 7:21.

ORDINARY TIME: WEEK 16B

Pondering Praise

Exodus 14:19–31; Psalm 105:1–6, 23–26, 45b;
Romans 14:1–12; Matthew 18:15–20

All: We dwell on the wondrous works of God and give praise to his holy name, pondering afresh his marvelous grace and liberating power. We gather as a people lost in awe.

Voice 1: Duplicity, argument, judgement, and disdain all spoil our praise refrain. But your grace frees us to restore, welcome, accept, and reconcile so that every tongue will praise your holy name.

Voice 2: Your grace gives us the freedom to accept the tension of difference that we bring so that everyone will stand together and praise your holy name.

All: We dwell on the wondrous works of God and give praise to his holy name, pondering afresh his marvelous grace and liberating power. We gather as a people lost in awe.

Voice 3: When we live for the Lord and not ourselves, our lives will become a song of praise. When we agree with thanks for your will to be done on earth, our sweet harmony will honor your holy name.

Prayers for the Season of Ordinary Time

Voice 4: Cloud by day, light by night tells the story of your protection and care. Just as walls of water let your people pass through the Red Sea, the Spirit guards our journey along the way. With mighty power, the Spirit sweeps away all who have evil intentions and refuse to praise your holy name.

All: We dwell on the wondrous works of God and give praise to his holy name, pondering afresh his marvelous grace and liberating power. We gather as a people lost in awe.

Voice 5: We remember all you have done, Lord. In Christ, you demonstrate your love for this world. We give you thanks for Jesus and praise your holy name.

Voice 6: As the Father of Abraham and Jacob, you demonstrate that your heart is for the poor. Through the Spirit, your promise to be with us forever. Together we praise your holy name.

All: We dwell on the wondrous works of God and give praise to his holy name, pondering afresh his marvelous grace and liberating power. We gather as a people lost in awe.

ORDINARY TIME: WEEK 17A

For the Sake of Your Name

Jeremiah 8:18–9:1; Psalm 79:1–9; 1 Timothy 2:1–7; Luke 16:1–13

All stand.

All: We rise to worship Jesus, our Lord,
the one mediator between all of us, who are bent toward sin, and the great love of God.

Women: For the sake of your name, weep with us in sorrow.
In solidarity with families in war zones, we plead for salvation.
Restore peace to all our lives so that we can live in goodness and dignity.

Men: For the sake of your name, weep with us in sorrow.
As human greed defiles your earth,
grip us all with repentance and restore your image in creation.

All sit.

All: We sit to lament the sins of your people—
the many ways we have amassed wealth and fail to live as your disciples.
For choosing to serve two masters, forgive us, Lord!

Women: For the sake of your name, weep with us in sorrow.
We lament the loss of faith in our time.
Because of our sins, we are a joke to our neighbors.
Hear our cry for all to be saved.

Prayers for the Season of Ordinary Time

Men: For the sake of your name, weep with us in sorrow.
We lament all abuse under the watch of the church.
We confess our many failures towards our indigenous brothers and sisters.
Let your compassion hurry to our neighborhood today.

All stand.

All: We rise to give thanks to Jesus, because you have set us free from sin and despair.
We surrender all that we have and all that we are to your service.

Leader: For the sake of your name, heal our wounds, restore our joy, and revive gospel hope throughout the whole earth.

All: Amen.

ORDINARY TIME: WEEK 17B

Praise for our Helper

*Esther 7:1–6, 9–10, 9:20–22; Psalm 124;
James 5:13–20; Mark 9:38–50*

People: In sickness and health, our life is in Christ. When torrents threaten us, your strong arm is sure to save. When raging waters drag us down, you are our helper. You meet us in our need.

Left: Lord, your desire is to give us life. Though some would treat us as slaves, we are not for sale in your eyes. If you weren't for us, our enemies would have swallowed us whole.

Right: Lord, your desire is to give us life. Though some try to tempt us, you keep our feet from slipping and falling into the snares of sin. If you weren't for us, our enemies would have swallowed us whole.

People: We are salted with fire, Lord, as we follow your cruciform way. When our sins would wipe us out, you help us, forgive us, and meet us in our need.

Left: Our help is in the name of the Lord. When we were sick, you empowered our brothers and sisters, leaders and friends to pray for us. By your Spirit, you healed us. If you weren't for us, sickness would have swallowed us whole.

Prayers for the Season of Ordinary Time

Right: Our help is in the name of the Lord. When violence threatened our homes and neighborhoods, we pleaded our cause before you. If you weren't for us, violence would have swallowed us whole.

People: Bless the Lord, the Maker of heaven and earth.
Bless the Lord, who didn't hand our lives over to evil.
Bless the Lord, who companions us with friends who are for us.
Bless the Lord, who gives us the gifts of salvation, forgiveness, and peace.
Bless the Lord, who refreshes us in Christ.
All praise to Jesus, our helper, who meets us in our need.

ORDINARY TIME: WEEK 18A

Enabled for a Sacrament of Praise

Exodus 17:1–4; Psalm 78:1–4, 12–16;
Philippians 2:1–13; Matthew 21:23–32

All stand.

All: We cry out to the Lord in the joy of new life. Through the Spirit, empower our lives to mirror the way of our self-giving Savior.

Women: You enable us to live out your good purposes in the world.

Men: You enable us to walk the cruciform way of Christ.

Leader: Unite us in Christ. When we stumble, quarrel, or complain, direct us to Jesus, the source of our new life.

All sit.

All: We cry out to the Lord in the joy of new life. Through the Spirit, testify to the power of your love working in our lives, the witness of church, our fellowship with one another, and the living voice of Scripture.

Women: Through the amazing comfort of your love, you enable us to live through dry seasons. When we doubt your presence, you remind us that you are Lord of all.

Men: You enable us to love one another as brothers and sisters in Christ. When our pride pushes back against your authority, you remind us of your humility on the cross and the empty tomb.

Prayers for the Season of Ordinary Time

Leader: You enable us to be your body, bending our ears toward your truth and nourishing us with Scripture and the crowd of witnesses in your world.

All stand.

All: We cry out to the Lord in the joy of new life. Through your Spirit, we encounter your presence at the table you prepared for us. As we remember your miraculous power, deliverance, and healing, may we fall on our knees and worship.

Women: As you lead us out of our slavery to sin and oppression, may we make room for the poor at this meal and honor your liberating heart.

Men: As we gather as your church, may our life together flow like a river from your Spirit, bringing justice, peace, and hope into the world.

Leader: Through this meal, you enable us to become a community of faith that seeks to serve the world. We hold your dove of peace in our hand, your reconciling love in our heart, and your generous welcome that embraces all.

All: As we share this meal, may we live out a good future, for when we gather in Christ, you are with us. Hallelujah!

ORDINARY TIME: WEEK 18B

Come Near to God

Proverbs 31:10-31; Psalm 1; James 3:13—4:3, 7-8a; Mark 9:30-37

People: Praise God, who knows every move we make and cheers us on in Christ. God smiles at the details of our faith, hope, and love. When we submit to his embrace, he gives us the authority to resist temptation.

Leader: Come near to God, and he will come near to you. Rejoice today and in him be glad.

People: When we trust our hearts to God, he fires our imaginations and brings good into our lives. Praise his name!

Leader: Come near to God, and she will come near to you. Rejoice today and in her be glad.

People: Happy people love God's instruction and let God's word come alive in their hearts. They do not follow advice from those who sit in disrespect or linger in doubt. They are planted in Christ by the waters of life.

Leader: Come near to God, and he will come near to you. Rejoice today and in him be glad.

People: Christ stands between us and the world as a source of great light. Christ calls us to walk in humility and to act for the good. But when we pursue selfish ambition, we deny the truth.

Leader: Come near to God, and she will come near to you. Rejoice today in her be glad.

People:	Christ teaches us to welcome all who are despised and rejected by the world. In the resurrected power and wisdom of Christ, we are filled with mercy, and we can make peace with those around us and work for the good. As we surrender to Christ, we will become more pure, gentle, obedient, fair, and genuine.
Leader:	Come near to God, and Christ will come near to you. Rejoice today and in Christ be glad. Amen.

ORDINARY TIME: WEEK 19A

Perseverance

*Exodus 33:12–23; Psalm 99; 1 Thessalonians 1:1–10;
Matthew 22:15–22*

All:	For your self-giving love and forgiveness through Christ, receive our praise.
Leader:	We turn from the idols that enchant us to exalt and praise your holy name.
Right:	We love to tell the story of your wide welcome, an open door in good times and bad. Hallelujah!
Left:	We love to tell the story of your grace and peace, which are beacons through the struggles of life. Hallelujah!
All:	For your self-giving love and forgiveness through Christ, receive our praise.
Leader:	We turn from the idols that enchant us to exalt and praise your holy name.
Right:	We love to tell the story of how you came to us through Christ, your Son, and provide all that we need through his grace. Hallelujah!
Left:	We love to tell the story of your faithful and impartial love for us through Christ. Hallelujah!
All:	For your self-giving love and forgiveness through Christ, receive our praise.
Leader:	We turn from the idols that enchant us to exalt and praise your holy name.

Right: We love to tell the story of your coming kingdom, when all will be blessed before your presence. We want to know you, seek your ways, and follow your commands for our lives. Hallelujah!

Left: We love to tell the story of your sweet justice, goodness, kindness, and compassion for the whole world. We want to proclaim your great name forever and ever. Hallelujah!

All: For your self-giving love and forgiveness through Christ, we exalt and praise your holy name. Hallelujah! Hallelujah!

ORDINARY TIME: WEEK 19B

Salvation Praise

Exodus 32:1–14; Psalm 106:1–6, 19–23;
Philippians 14:1–9; Matthew 22:1–14

Leader: Lord, we confess that we are ruining everything you have made. We have embraced sin by trying to determine our own futures. But in Jesus, you remember us with love, and so we give you thanks.

Women: Lord, you created us in your image, but we have followed selfish interests by trying to go our own way. Yet in Jesus, you remember your faithful and self-giving love for all things, and so we give you thanks.

Men: Lord, we have forged comfortable idols and hitched our pride to the wagons of financial success, physical prowess, and technological assets. Yet Christ reveals our hollow lives and calls us to a life of freedom as we follow him, and so we give you thanks.

Leader: Praise the Lord, who visits us with salvation through Christ. You choose to embrace us through your Son and bring joy into our hearts. Through Christ, you have entered the world in gentleness and remain near to us. Hallelujah!

Women: Through Christ, you free our hearts and minds from anxieties and worries. Through the Spirit, we can focus on all that is excellent, admirable, true, and just. Hallelujah!

Prayers for the Season of Ordinary Time

Men: Through Christ, the lamb who was slain, you have put your anger far from us. Through the Holy Spirit, you visit us, comfort us, and empower us to uphold justice and to live pure and righteous lives. Hallelujah!

Leader: You liberate us from violence in our homes and distress about the state of our world. When we are groaning cogs in the corporate machine or terrified by the captains of war, your arm is strong to save.

Women: You invite us to a party of grace and guide our feet along the path of peace.

Men: You shower us with joy and fill us with the desire to be your willing servants as we seek to love our neighbors. Send us to the margins so that we can invite all to your glorious celebration.

All: With Christ as our advocate. We praise your name. Amen.

ORDINARY TIME: WEEK 20A

The Beauty of the Earth in the Light of Christ

Job 1:1, 2:1–10; Psalm 26; Hebrews 1:1–4, 2:5–12; Mark 10:2–16

People: Brother sun, sister moon, join with earth and sky to declare the creative, sustaining love of God for the world. A gentle breeze of your Spirit nourishes hope, which issues in a cosmically diverse song of joy.

Leader: Through Jesus, the light of God's glory, the world was created. We bear the image of our Creator—Father, Son, and Spirit.

All: Hallelujah!

People: From the rising of the sun to its setting, all creation breaks out in praise to the Creator, the cosmic sustainer of the whole world.

Leader: God speaks to us through his Son, Jesus, who repairs the world's breaches and makes all things new. Christ welcomes all humanity and all the creatures of the earth into his kingdom.

All: Hallelujah!

People: For the earth's thick canopy, which provides rich bounty for the whole creation, we offer astonished praise. For the great networks of rivers, lakes, and seas that provide water for us to drink, we give joyful praise. For all wildlife, great and small, and for our pets, creatures of loyal love, we give heartfelt thanks.

Prayers for the Season of Ordinary Time

Leader: As stewards of all that God has made, our calling is to honor the image of God within us, all peoples, the global community, and the beauty of his creation all around us. We praise Christ, who mends our brokenness and restores creation to its full glory.

All: Hallelujah!

People: We want to be faithful stewards of your creation, and so we turn from evil ways, exploitive practices, and any selfish desire that threatens our biosphere. We cry out for you to restrain those who remain thoughtless, indifferent, and destructive to your creation. Expose the slick talk of untamed economic growth. Protect your world, its people, and all life forms under the shadow of your wings.

Leader: Praise God, who loves the vast cosmic sweep of creation and beckons us to care for his world.

All: Hallelujah!

People: Praise God for all who are committed to climate mitigation, animal husbandry, and the regeneration of scarred landscapes.

Leader: Praise God for his good world of plenty, which brings us delight and joy. Praise God for our salvation in Jesus, the pioneer of our redeemed calling.

All: Hallelujah!

ORDINARY TIME: WEEK 20B

A Full Voice Declaration

Job 1:1, 2:1–10; Psalm 26; Hebrews 1:1–4, 2:5–12; Mark 10:2–16

All:	On the level ground at the cross of Christ, we behold your faithful love and declare together, "Bless the Lord our God!"[1]
Men:	God has spoken to his people through the prophets in many times and many ways.
Women:	God has spoken to us through his son, Jesus, who cleanses us from sin.
Leader:	Jesus sits at the right hand of God's majesty and is crowned with glory and honor.
All:	On the level ground at the cross of Christ, we behold our Savior and proclaim together, "Bless the Lord our God!"
Men:	You have established order and justice in your creation and have set us in families. Forgive us when we seek to pull apart what you have put together. Preserve our lives and heal our land.
Women:	You have redeemed the world through your Son. Forgive us when our hearts are hard and we do not yield to your self-giving love. Strengthen our community and reconcile our relationships with our neighbors.
Leader:	Jesus is the imprint of God's being, the light of God's glory, the heir of all things.

---

1. Ps 26:12.

Prayers for the Season of Ordinary Time

All: On the level ground at the cross of Christ, we behold our Savior and proclaim together, "Bless the Lord our God!"

Men: You promise not to let your world spin out of control. Forgive us when we fail to see your grace amidst our distress. Help us to trust you and to receive both good and bad from your hands.[2]

Women: Through Jesus, you set us free from slavery, and so we no longer need to fear death. Forgive us when we fail to walk in your truth and follow selfish desires and pursuits that are bringing death to your world. Help us join together to accept your call to steward the creation.

Leader: Father, Son, and Spirit, you are never silent. In Jesus, we see the fullness of your glory.

All: On the level ground at the cross of Christ, we behold our Savior and proclaim together, "Bless the Lord our God!"

---

2. Job 2:10.

ORDINARY TIME: WEEK 21A

Faithful Harmony Praise

*Exodus 20:1–4, 7–9, 12–20; Psalm 19;
Philippians 3:4b–14; Matthew 21:33–46*

Leader: Jesus is the cornerstone of the church and the life of the world. His death on a cross and his resurrection glory have brought our redemption. We surrender to you, Lord Christ, in love.

Men: We have written off our assets for the sake of knowing you.

Women: Your grace and beauty are amazing in our eyes.

Leader: God, you know our world spirals from one day to the next in racial, economic, moral, and societal distress. Forgive our sins and revive our hearts so that we can follow your way of love into the world.

Men: We trust in your faithfulness and self-giving love, Jesus.

Women: We delight to know you, Christ, and the power of your resurrection.

Leader: Thank you, God, that you have found us in Christ. Help us to embrace the cruciform way of your son, Jesus, so that we can join you in your suffering as we seek to love the world around us. We hear the cries of the poor and broken-hearted, those who are abused and alone. We see the unemployed, oppressed, and vilified. Stir our hearts to respond with justice and compassion.

Prayers for the Season of Ordinary Time

Men: Father of our Lord Jesus Christ, we have no other God before you. Your loving commands are sweet, like honey dripping from a honeycomb.

Women: You are loyal and gracious to all who love you and keep your commandments.

Leader: God, we trust that the whole world is in your hands. We pray for our community and all its services, schools, aged care and health facilities, businesses, and all who make this place their home. Scatter us as agents of your reconciliation.

All: May the words of our mouths and the meditations of our hearts be pleasing to you, O
Lord, our rock and our redeemer!

ORDINARY TIME: WEEK 21B

Pattern Recognition Praise

Lamentations 1:1–6, 3:19–26; 2 Timothy 1:1–14; Luke 17:5–10

All stand.

People: Praise God, whose faithful love will endure forever. Praise Jesus, the Son, whose life, death, and resurrection bring the promise of new life for all. Praise the Spirit, who tenderly cares for God's good creation.

Leader: We praise you for the gospel of Christ, which extends through time, declaring your purpose and grace for creation.

People: We thank you for your hospitality in inviting us to meet with you in the sharing of bread and wine. We recognize you afresh today.

Leader: We pray for the difficulties facing your church as we acknowledge the cruciform pattern of the gospel. Help us to share in your suffering for the sake of the world, and may our praise affirm our embrace of the gospel.

All sit.

People: Lord, we confess that we feel alone as we face the struggles of our time.
We want to trust your will for our lives, but we are tired and depleted.
The whole creation is on edge.
Our faith lacks imagination, and we are failing to love our neighbors as ourselves.

Prayers for the Season of Ordinary Time

Leader: Though we are like a deer panting for water in the wilderness, depressed and overwhelmed by the suffering around us, we trust that your love will renew us and your compassion will strengthen us to face each new day.
We praise you for your faithfulness.

All stand.

People: Lord, we we wait for your deliverance.
We ask you to remember to do good to all who hope in you and seek your face.
In your grace and mercy, heal our lands.
Give us your peace as we look to you as the bread of life, our true vine.

Leader: As your humble servants, we ask you to increase our faith so that we can praise you with joy. Today our prayer is an endorsement of "the pattern of sound teaching" and the gifts of faith.[1] Empower us by the Holy Spirit so that we can love the world around us with the self-giving love of Christ.

All: Amen.

---

1. 1 Tim 1:13.

ORDINARY TIME: WEEK 22A

A Song of Praise for Followers of Jesus

Jeremiah 29:1, 4–7; Psalm 66:1–12; 2 Timothy 2:8–15; Luke 17:11–19

All:	We come together as followers of Jesus, who calls us to die to selfish ambition and live in his resurrection power.
Women:	God's word reminds us that we can accept times of testing as we pass through fire and water because Jesus is with us, and you, Father, "will lead us to freedom."[1]
Men:	God's word reminds us that we can follow the call of Christ through trials and sufferings, which increase our faith and endurance, because all who put their hope in Christ will find he remains faithful.[2]
All:	Together, we call on all the earth to sing with joy to you, O God, who creates, heals, and saves. *(Clap clap.)*
Women:	God keeps a good eye on the nations and knows when his people are living as outcasts in exile, desperate for his mercy and healing.
Men:	In Jesus, God travels the borders,[3] seeking the lepers, outcasts, and marginalized. We pray for your mercy upon all who are lost today as we return to you this song of praise.

---

1. Ps 66:12.
2. 2 Tim 2:10, 13.
3. Luke 17:11

Prayers for the Season of Ordinary Time

All: Together, we sing praise to you, O Lord, for your awesome works, great strength, and the healing power of Christ, our Good Shepherd, who transforms our lives. *(Clap clap.)*

Women: As followers of Jesus, together we seek to live as a multicultural community in our time, sowing seeds of peace rather than war, harmony rather than intolerance, and gentleness rather than violence.

Men: As followers of Jesus, together we seek the welfare of our cities, towns, and regions.11 In the name of Jesus, we work humbly for justice and mercy.

All: Together, we sing with joy and praise you, Father, Son, and Spirit,
so that all the earth will come to bless your name.
Amen. *(Clap, Clap.)*

ORDINARY TIME: WEEK 22B

Praise for the Renewing Word of God

Jeremiah 31:27–34; Psalm 119:97–104;
2 Timothy 3:14–4:5, Luke 18:1–8

Left: We announce the praise of our lips for you, God, the Creator of all.

Right: We beckon all who know you, from the least to the greatest, to bless your name, the word of life.

Left: Comfort us with the imprint of your word in our hearts.

Right: You promise to bring justice for all who cry out to your name.

Left: When you forgive our sins, we are filled with everlasting joy;.

Right: When we surrender to your love, you faithfully fill us with hope.

Left: Give us the seed of Christ so that we might grow in grace. Amen!

Right: Instruct, inspire, and ignite power in our lives through your word.

Left: Your presence, Jesus, helps us endure suffering and adversity.

Right: As we contemplate your word and keep its instruction, your love grows in us and gives us self-control.

Left: Your commands lead us away from evil and guide us on your path.

Prayers for the Season of Ordinary Time

Right: Nothing can hold back your love to the world in Christ Jesus. Nothing!

Left: Open our eyes so that we can see your good future, the fruit of your gospel growing in our lives.

Right: Restore us by your word, correcting our self-centered ideas with your truth.

Left: Through the embrace of your covenant love, make us your instruments of your peace and praise.

Right: May we live to the rhythm of your grace through the encouragement of the Spirit.

Left: When we take our eyes off the living word, Jesus, draw us back into fellowship with you.

Right: You are the eternal Word, and we long to worship in the presence of your abiding light and love forever and ever.

All: Amen.

ORDINARY TIME: WEEK 23A

Finishing Line Praise

Joel 2:23–32; Psalm 65; 2 Timothy 4:6–8, 16–18; Luke 18:9–14

Leader: We set our hearts on waiting for your presence, O Lord, delighted to come together to offer you our prayer and praise.

People: You soften our hearts with showers of your love as the gateways of morning and evening sing for joy.
Pour your Spirit upon us so that our lives will be fruitful in your kingdom.

Leader: Forgive our sins and protect us from self-righteousness as we cry out, "God, show mercy to me, a sinner."[1]

People: You bring down the proud and liberate us through the cruciform love of Christ. By your spirit, help us to fight the good fight, finish the race in joy, and keep the faith.[2]

Leader: When we pass through the wilderness, we will wait for your Spirit to bring growth, new visions, and dreams. May even the silence of fierce landscapes praise you.

People: Lord, you call us to embrace the way of the cross. As we follow you on this path, thank you for walking with, ahead of, and behind us. We praise you because your raw power is resolved in tension with your presence for peace.

---

1. Luke 18:13.
2. 2 Tim 4:7.

Prayers for the Season of Ordinary Time

Leader: As we walk with you, all creation breaks out in songs of praise, for you are at the center of the universe and also on the margins. Hallelujah!

People: We will sing your song, Father, Son, and Spirit, until we cross the finish line. Give us strength so that we can preach the great gospel of Christ Jesus to all the nations, for the sake of your kingdom glory.

All: In the name of Jesus, Amen!

ORDINARY TIME: WEEK 23B

Leaping, Bounding Praise

Habakkuk 1:1–4, 2:1–4; Psalm 119:137–144;
2 Thessalonians 1:1–4; 1:11–12; Luke 19:1–10

Leader: All praise to our cruciform God, the leader of the pack. You desire to bring salvation to every household and community. With leaping, bounding praise, we adore you.

Children: We are becoming children of faith. Meet us at our level so we don't have to climb trees to see you.

Adults: The stress and strain of daily life catches us off guard. Yet we hold onto the vision of your kingdom coming in Jesus, who showers us with grace.

Children: We know your rules for life will help us understand how to live and grow in leaps and bounds.

Adults: We thank you for the growing family of faith—old and young, You gather your people from every tribe and tongue so that we can grow in leaps and bounds of love for and with each other.

Children: We thank you for the adults in our lives who pray for us. Bless our family, and our church.

Adults: Sometimes we cry out for your help, and you don't seem to hear us. Don't you see the violence of war among nations and in our homes? Don't you see the unfairness and injustice in our world? Please come to us and work your righteousness among us, Lord God.

Children:	We jump for joy in your love, and so we want to do what is good.
All:	As sinners and saints, adults and children, we come before you as your guests. With leaping, bounding praise, we celebrate and honor your name. Amen.

ORDINARY TIME: WEEK 24A

All Saints Prayer

Revelation 7:9–17; Psalm 34:1–10, 22; 1 John 3:1–3; Matthew 5:1–12

All:	We come to praise you, Father, Son, and Spirit. We gather with the communion of saints, the great crowd of witnesses past and present, to bless the Lord, the great "I am"![1] We cheer for your coming kingdom.
Women:	"I sought the Lord and he answered me. He delivered me from all my fears."[2]
Men:	In our suffering and distress, we cry out to the Lord, who listens to us and saves us from every trouble.
Leader:	"The Lord saves the lives of his servants, all those who take refuge in him will not be condemned."[3]
All:	Our hearts are secure in the love of God. With joy and hope, we come together as friends, sisters, and brothers from every tribe and nation, every voice and language. We want to sing praises to our God and be in that number when the saints go marching in.
Women:	Victory belongs to the Lamb, who sits on the throne.
Men:	We embrace the cruciform victory of Jesus over sin and death, principalities and powers, sickness, suffering, and despair.

1. Ex 3:14.
2. Ps 34:4.
3. Ps 34:22.

Prayers for the Season of Ordinary Time

Leader: We embrace Jesus, our Shepherd, who leads us to springs of life-giving water and transforms our lives into the life of Christ.

All: Father, your love adopts us as your children. We are bursting with the hope of all you will do through us in your world today.

Women: In our world of suffering and distress, many are dying, but "the victory over sin and suffering belongs to the lamb on the throne."[4]

Men: The groans of grief are not far away, but you promise that you will wipe away every tear from our eyes and make our faces to shine.[5]

Leader: As we follow Christ, who is merciful, may our lives be known for mercy.

All: We seek to be your peacemakers and to bless the world around us as we joyfully seek your coming kingdom on earth as it is in heaven.

Women: You call us to endure as earth keepers in a time of serious soil erosion, depleting biodiversity, and climate crisis.

Men: You call us to be merciful to all who are suffering mental illness, hunger, homelessness, or financial ruin.

All: Through the Spirit-infused power of the resurrected Christ, make us a communion of saints who are pure in heart and committed to righteousness, justice, and the way of the cross.

---

4. Rev 7:10.
5. Rev 21:4.

ORDINARY TIME: WEEK 24B

All Saint's Chant for Praise

Isaiah 25:6–9; Psalm 24; Revelations 21:1–6a; John 11:32–44

All: Lift your heads up, people of God. Shout out his praise! It is time for a beautiful bride, your church, to join the feast of heaven.

Right: Christ has swallowed up death forever and removed the disgrace of our sins. Hallelujah!

Left: God will wipe away all tears from our eyes. The former heaven and earth will pass away, and there will be no more mourning, crying, or pain anymore. Hallelujah!

All: Lift your heads up, people of God. Shout out his praise!

Right: The gaze of Jesus rests on all his saints. Through Christ, God is with us, and we will see his glory.

Left: "The earth is the Lord's and everything in it."[6] God, who has established the land, sea, and sky, ushers us into his presence through the grace of Christ.

All: Lift your heads up, people of God. Shout out his praise!

Right: We have waited for your salvation, O Lord. On this happy day, we will be glad and rejoice with all your saints as they go marching into your kingdom.

Left: Your love saves all generations from the smell of death. In resurrection power, you have removed our hearts of stone. The whole earth is ready to praise you!

---

6. Ps 24:1.

Prayers for the Season of Ordinary Time

All: Lift your heads up, people of God. Shout out his praise!

Right: In Christ alone, our salvation is sure. We give you thanks for your mercy and for your faithful presence here with us.

Left: Through Christ, you dwell with your creation. You are the Alpha and Omega, the beginning and end of our joy, the resounding voice of grace for all saints.

All: Lift your heads up, people of God. Shout out his praise!

ORDINARY TIME: WEEK 25A

Praise to the God Who Comes Near

Joshua 3:7–17; Psalm 107:1–7, 33–37;
Matthew 23:1–12; 1 Thessalonians 2:9–13

All: We come together to thank the Lord for his faithful love. All glory and honor to the God who comes near and speaks to us in his Son!

Right: From the east and west, north and south, you call near all who have been redeemed in Christ to praise you, our Father and ruler of the universe!

Left: We praise you for saving us from sin and liberating us from our enemies. You have drawn freely in your "covenant chest" of love.[7]

Right: We leave behind the desert places of our hearts and seek the call of your cruciform kingdom. By your Spirit, empower us to walk the talk.

Left: Dress us in the humility of Jesus, our one true teacher, and free us from our heavy burdens so that we can work together as brothers and sisters of your coming kingdom.[8]

All: You love a crowded table, where diversity is sustained through grace. As we share this meal today, may we honor your generous welcome and bear witness to your

---

7. Josh 3:3.
8. Matt 23:10.

loving presence among us. All praise to the God who comes near.

Right: As we gather around your broken body, the bread of your generous new creation, may we hunger and thirst for what is right and good, the day when justice will roll down like waters, your righteousness like a rushing stream.

Left: As we gather around this wine, which has been crafted through your self-giving love for the world, satisfy us and remind us that we bear your image into the world.

Right: On this day, may the love between Father, Son, and Spirit overflow to our generation.

Left: On this day, may our hospitality touch the lives of our neighbors and the created world around us.

Right: On this day, we remember your gracious provision with gratitude

Left: On this day, we invite your Spirit to empower us so that we can go out into the world to plant the gospel and look forward to a fruitful harvest.

All: We come together to thank the Lord for his faithful love. All glory and honor to the God who comes near and speaks to us through his Son! Amen.

ORDINARY TIME: WEEK 25B

Praise for Jesus, who has the Power to Heal and Save

1 Samuel 1:4–20, 2:1–10; Hebrews 10:11–14, 19–25; Mark 13:1–8

People: In times of war and rumors of war, we cannot stop crying. It is difficult to praise you with a lump in our throat. But then you intervene and turn around our alarm, and we rest in your peace and worship you with songs of praise.

Women: When others make fun of us and we feel like we are at the center of relentless bullying, we cry out for you to deliver us. But then you hear us and provide shelter for us beneath the shadow of your wings, where we praise your good and holy name.

Men: When the proud speak evil about us and ridicule you for being a God who cannot act, we cry out for you to remember us. But then you redeem us, our rock and our strong redeemer, and our hearts rejoice in your goodness.

Leader: Praise our God, who keeps his promises forever and centers us in his love.

People: We are ready to serve you in faith, hope and love. When the deceiver comes, correct our visions and dreams so that we will worship you alone forever.

Women: Remember your servants, Lord. Protect us from deception and rescue us when are crushed and despairing. In you alone, we put our trust.

Prayers for the Season of Ordinary Time

Men: Remember your servants, Lord. When we are vulnerable and exposed, lift us up and cover us with your love and grace. In you alone, we put our trust.

Leader: As servants of your love, we are willing to make sacrifices for your kingdom. But Jesus, we need your strength to sustain us.

People: Through Christ alone, fire our imagination with your love and motivate us by your Spirit to bless and serve our neighbors and the world around us.

Women: Shatter the strength of coercive power in our homes so that they can be places of safety and love, where we can praise your name.

Men: Look and see your people's pain, Lord. We could hide in a haze of beer and wine, but we are praying. Out of times of great worry and trouble, hear the cry of our hearts for your salvation and grace.

Leader: We worship the name of Jesus, who is mighty to heal and save.

People: In your mercy, raise up the poor from the dust and guide us into a new way of living, where there is plenty for all.

Women: Lamb of God who takes away the sin of the world, we draw near to you with genuine thanksgiving for your loving sacrifice for all.

Men: You are the ruler over all the corners of the earth, and your name has been raised high above every other name. You alone have the power to heal and save. To you, alone, we give our full-hearted praise.

All: Hallelujah! Hallelujah!

ORDINARY TIME: WEEK 26A

Praise to the Lord, who Hears our Lament

Judges 4:1–7; Psalm 125; 1 Thessalonians 5:1–11; Matthew 25:14–30

Leader: We cry out to you, Lord, in our day of distress. Have you given us over to those who do evil? Have you become impatient with us? The whole world is caught in the trap of fear. We gasp and groan like a woman in labor.

All: Hear our cry, Lord. Hear our cry.

Leader: Lord, the darkness is driving many to drown their sorrows. In this time of self-isolation, we seem to be buried in a graceless world, where there is no end to the weeping. We are caught off guard by the threat of sudden destruction, the thief who has come in the night to plunder and steal.

All: Hear our cry, Lord, and return to your people.

Leader: Send your Spirit among us again as we cry out for your hurting world. Rescue us from the power of evildoers. Shine the light of Jesus into this enveloping darkness so that all can see your goodness and grace.

All: Hear our cry, Lord, and remember the salvation you offer to all through Jesus.

Leader: In our distress, as we suffer in the grip of evil, restore your stability and peace among us. Set our hearts on Jesus so that we can be faithful servants in his kingdom of justice and peace.

Prayers for the Season of Ordinary Time

All: Hear our cry, Lord, and surround us with your love and hope.

Leader: We praise you, Lord, for all our brothers and sisters who are active in reconciling this world to you. Empower us through the gospel of Christ so that we can encourage one another through these dark days.

All: You hear us, Jesus! *(Clap clap clap.)*
You hear us, Jesus! *(Clap clap clap.)*
Thank you, Jesus! *(Clap clap clap.)*

ORDINARY TIME: WEEK 26B

Praise for Jesus, the One We Love

1 Samuel 1:4–20, 2:1–10; Hebrews 10:11–25; Mark 13:1–8

People: O Lord, we praise you for the great love you showed the whole world through Jesus.

Women: When you see our pain and distress, remember to lift us up and to remove our sins through the cross-shaped love of your Son.

Men: When you see our sad and barren lives, remember to lift us up and to remove our sins through the cross-shaped love of your Son.

Leader: Jesus Christ, our high priest, has offered himself as a sacrifice for all sins, once for all time.

People: Praise to you, Lord Christ, for you are delivering us from fear and evil.

Women: Through the Spirit, place your laws in our hearts so that we can be transformed into your likeness.

Men: Through the Spirit, write your laws on our minds so that we can be transformed into your likeness.

Leader: Through the resurrection power of Christ, may God transform us into the likeness of Jesus.

People: Strengthen our hearts to serve you, O Lord, to the far corners of the earth.

Women: You raise the poor from dust. You hear the cries of the poor and needy. You comfort all who are in distress.

Men:	You are a champion of justice. You bring down the proud and arrogant and raise up the lowly, who are confined to the garbage piles of life.
Leader:	O Lord, hear our prayers, which come from our heart with tears. Where the wicked are dying in darkness, be the light of truth that leads to peace. Guard the feet of your faithful servants as they wash the feet of the world.
All:	As brothers and sisters united by faith and hope in Christ, we encourage each other to live in love and to do good works. Amen.

ORDINARY TIME—CHRIST THE KING SUNDAY: WEEK 27A

Praise for Christ the King

Jeremiah 23:1–6; Luke 1:68–79; Colossians 1:11–20; Luke 23:35–43

All:	Bless the Lord. *(Clap clap.)*
Leader:	Bless the Lord, the dawn from heaven, who breaks with compassion upon our world.
Left:	We bless the Lord, who has delivered his people by raising up a mighty Savior.
Right:	We bless the Lord, who has saved us from the reign of darkness and adopted us into his kingdom of love.
All:	Bless the Lord. *(Clap clap.)*
Leader:	Bless the Lord, who comes as a light to all who sit in darkness and live in the shadows of death.
Left:	We bless the Lord because no one needs to miss out, for Jesus alone can guide this world to the path of peace.
Right:	We bless the Lord, who speaks words of forgiveness to his enemies from the cross of Christ, and whose power of love reaches beyond sneering, mocking insults to enfold us all.
All:	Bless the Lord. *(Clap clap.)*
Leader:	Bless the Lord, who has shown mercy to the whole world, making peace through the self-giving love of Christ on the cross.

Prayers for the Season of Ordinary Time

Left: We bless the Lord Jesus, the first born from the dead, who has been given the exalted place over everything in the universe.

Right: We bless the Lord Jesus, whom we serve without fear, as we wait patiently for the fullness of God's kingdom to come on earth as it is in heaven!

All: Bless the Lord. *(Clap clap.)*

Leader: Bless the Lord, Christ the King, who gathers all who are lost in sin like scattered sheep. Bless the Lord, Christ the King, who is quick to save and gathers all who are lost into his strong and tender embrace so that no one will miss out on the action of God's kingdom of Love.

Left: Praise Christ the King. *(Clap clap.)*

Right: Praise Christ the King. *(Clap clap.)*

All: Praise Christ the King. *(Clap clap.)*

ORDINARY TIME—CHRIST THE KING SUNDAY: WEEK 27B

Christ is King

2 Samuel 23:1–7; Psalm 132:1–18; Revelation 1:4b–8; John 18:33–37

All who are mobile, move to the nearest entrance or doorway in the sanctuary.

Leader: Jesus Christ, the first born from among dead, we pronounce you as our King. You alone are the ruler over all the leaders of this world.

People: We are listening for your voice, Jesus, for you alone testify to the truth, which is a lamp that helps us find our way.
Take four steps toward the leader and halt.

Leader: Jesus Christ, we pronounce you as our King. With the Father and the Spirit, you are the Alpha and Omega, the almighty God who was and is to come.

People: We are listening for your voice, Jesus, for you alone have been sent by the God who was and is and is to come. You are our Creator and Redeemer, our King in resurrection glory.
Take four steps toward the leader and halt.

Leader: Jesus Christ, we pronounce you as our King. You came into the world as a humble servant, a martyr of the truth of God's love. As our resurrected King, come quickly and establish your kingdom in this world!

People: We are listening for your voice, Jesus, for the saints sing for joy in your presence, and your kingdom is not of this world. You promise to satisfy the poor, lonely, and broken-hearted with food that lasts. You delight to bless us with your abundance forever.

All move to the space around the leader.

Leader: Jesus Christ, we pronounce you as our King. You did not come into the world to rule over others in power but to serve the world in love. As our servant King, release us from the "will to power" and transform us into your likeness.

People: We are listening for your voice, Jesus, for you are our King, who satisfies all our needs. We trust the future of our lives and world in your strong hands of love.

Leader: Jesus Christ, we pronounce you as our King. You alone deliver us from sin and defeat every altar we have made to evil in our lives. We hear the words, "your sins are forgiven," with joyful gratitude. May we, who have freely received, be people who freely give in your name.

All: We are listening for your gentle voice, Jesus, for you have freed us from our debt to sin, and we are ready to affirm your great love for the whole world as your ambassadors, O Christ, our King. *(Shout)* Amen!

Postface

Life comes with the ebbs and flows of bad times and good. As we look back at the COVID-19 pandemic, we face the sober recognition of lives lost and the wide-ranging medical, social economic, and political consequences that have caused distress. We have all been touched by grief and loss.

For many, the pandemic exposed our dependence on the coherence, stability, and predictable goodness of life. This unexpected disorientation has resulted in anguish as well as creative engagement, a trigger for new energy and imagination across communities and churches.

I also recognize two other forces that have been at play. First, the pandemic has challenged the prevailing worldviews of autonomy and individualism. Loneliness became a crisis for many, and new expressions of community and the body of Christ have emerged. Second, the background prevalence of apocalyptic thinking is significant in our world, and the pandemic brought to the surface fears and conversations about a time of sudden dislocation and judgement for the sins that support our contemporary status quo. Both within and outside of the church, fears about personal restraint, conspiratorial thinking around vaccination programs, and reactions to heavy-handed political social controls have emerged.

At the same time, some genuine good has accompanied this global pathogen event. We have slowed down, enjoyed longer family and neighborly time, planted gardens, and completed long-needed home maintenance. But as it happens, other bad times have also emerged. Alcohol misuse and its consequences became apparent. Eating disorders and family-based violence both multiplied. Wars broke out in Ukraine and Myanmar, and there was a chaotic withdrawal of American troops from Afghanistan. Issues around entrenched racism exposed problematic policing. Calls for freedom provided an opportunity for women to speak about unwanted sexual violence and more.

POSTFACE

This collection of "new normal" prayers developed in such a time. They capture something of the pressures we faced together as well as those of my own context as a doctor, family member, local community citizen, and member of my faith community.

In writing this collection of prayers, I can recognize the following. First, writing the prayers became a spiritual practice, where I brought the existential challenges of this time to encounter Scripture, which resulted in a dynamism in the prayers. Each prayer took around two hours to write, and I found that through this focused immersion, God sustained me for frontline Covid demands.

Second, these prayers were an act of service for my congregational brothers and sisters. Offline or online, we prayed together through the light of Scripture as it is arranged in the liturgical year and through the threatening darkness of our bad times. We shared the need to express lament in tension while offering thanks for God's continued blessings. Then we offered both in the presence of God as worship. Some prayers reflect our attempts as a congregation to adjust to new forms of the sacrament of communion. Some prayers reach into other circles of Christian fellowship. As Bonhoeffer noted during his time of global crisis, "True prayer does not depend either on individuals or the whole body of the faithful, but solely upon the knowledge that our heavenly Father knows our needs."[1] And again, "corporate prayer, offered in the name of Christ, is the purest form of fellowship."[2]

Third, Bonhoeffer has been a mentor in his encouragement that "intercession is the most promising way to reach our neighbors."[3] This pandemic has roused many cries of lament within our communities. The pandemic has been a serious time to love our neighbors as ourselves. Even in times of shutdown, all people of faith could recognize the suffering and anguish of the people around us, and so these prayers sought to give voice to the multiple needs in both local and global communities. Writing these prayers became a time of learning as I sought to bring our world's suffering to God through cries of lament and intercession. My sense is that lament has, for the most part, been ignored in modern Western worship, and so I needed to learn the structure of these prayers, which are patterned after

---

1. Bonhoeffer, *Cost of Discipleship*, 147.
2. Bonhoeffer, *Cost of Discipleship*, 88.
3. Bonhoeffer, *Cost of Discipleship*, 88.

the Psalms—a cry, then a complaint, followed by a request, and concluding with an affirmation.

I grew in my own faith in this journey. Lament captured the angst and distress of many of my patients and also helped me manage the frustrations of conspiracy theories and pushback against sensible health prevention measures. In *Risking Truth: Reshaping the World through Prayers of Lament*, Scott Ellington speaks of lament's spiritual power. He writes, "Each event in Israel's history occurs within the flow of a continuous relationship, and when a past event is re-presented in a lament in the present, past and present are joined as God responds to that prayer."[4]

Ellington wrestles with the apparent silence of God in the face of the cries of suffering. He observes, "By insisting that experiences in the present be integrated with their salvation story, Israel places their core story endlessly at risk, while at the same time making possible a fresh owning of that story by new generations."[5] Lament takes us to very deep wells of God's love and grace.

Yet lament is not a panacea for suffering. Rather, such prayers can give words to the feeling that it is "possible we have 'fallen out of' the story of those for whom God acts to save."[6] Laments allow us to face the moments when we ask, "is it finally over?" amidst the darkness of suffering.[7]

Fourth, one of the surprises within any experience of suffering are the moments of grace, random acts of kindness, and compassion. With the seeing eyes and hearing ears of faith, chords of thankful praise can emerge. As we break into thankfulness, we are relieved from the ongoing wrestle of suffering as we can finally hear "God singing over us" in love.[8] To be led by the Spirit from lament to gratefulness and praise is a gift that we can learn on the way as we walk with Christ through both bad times and good.

Fifth, as I reflect on my unexpected entry into the world of biblical poetry and poetry itself, I can recognize an initial prompting of the Spirit. I could have written prayers for myself and others, but by linking these prayers to the liturgical cycles of Scripture—the whole counsel of God, as it were—they become prayers of the people of God.

4. Ellington, *Risking Truth*, 87.
5. Ellington, *Risking Truth*, 87.
6. Ellington, *Risking Truth*, 87.
7. Ellington, *Risking Truth*, 89.
8. Zeph 3:17b.

I can also recognize that I was motivated by a desire for comprehensive integrity. As humans, we can hold on to favored parts of the whole story of God while ignoring others. Yet it is dangerous to try to move forward without the balance, the winged keel, of the whole canon of Scripture. As the canonical scholar Brevard S. Childs notes, "Both testaments make a discrete witness to Jesus Christ which must be heard both separately and in concert."[9] Childs suggests that we engage Scripture as a dialogue—a dialectic between the witness of the biblical text and the reality of our lives, woven together by the Spirit. As he puts it, "Namely Jesus Christ is made active in constantly fresh forms of applications."[10] In this canonical, liturgical context, Jesus and his kingdom come into focus in both bad times and good.

Sixth, a strong theme that comes through many of these prayers is the self-giving love of God in Christ. I recognize here the impact of reading Michael Gorman's book, *Participating in Christ*. I sense this book has profound implications for the faith of all modern Christians as Gorman calls Christians to enter a cross-shaped spirituality and not simply rest on a forensic, cross-centered theology. Participation in Christ held a strong resonance for living by faith during the pandemic time and since. Many of these prayers are drawn from Paul's writings, poetry, and prayers. Gorman is a meticulous expositor, and many wonderful insights flow in his writing.

For Gorman, Philippians 2:5–11 is Paul's "master story" of self-giving love.[11] In exploring "kenosis," Gorman asserts that both the incarnation and the crucifixion represent the same mindset of God. This text in Philippians informs Paul's theology and spirituality, his living *in* Christ. Gorman compellingly concludes that "Paul's participatory spirituality is about self-giving love as sharing the very character and life of God."[12] Paul's spiritual life in Christ enabled him to follow Jesus through the most intense experiences of suffering, and I found this challenging to my faith—and also liberating as our world lived through the pandemic. The life of cross-shaped discipleship flows naturally into these prayers.

Seventh, these prayers keep the life, death and resurrection of Jesus in clear view. Jesus is the prism through which any lament, thanks, or praise flows. Bonhoeffer's phrase, "Christ stands between us and our neighbor,"

---

9. Quoted in Braun, *God's praise and God's presence*, 73.
10. Quoted in Braun, *God's praise and God's presence*, 74.
11. Gorman, *Participating in Christ*, 77.
12. Gorman, *Participating in Christ*, 95.

has been a groundswell for these prayers.[13] The pandemic has not been a time for judgement by Christians, but a time when Christ brings *everyone* into our field of fellowship. His love dispels all doubts about the "other." In prayers of lament and intercession, we express fellowship with all suffering humanity. With Christ, we are all in this together.

Walter Brueggemann's meditations from the psalms have also been a rich resource, and his connection to Mark 10 serves as a fitting conclusion: "God first wants not money but mouths—speech, utterance, testimony—to evoke new reality. And from such speech comes action in the world."[14]

---

13. Bonhoeffer, *Cost of Discipleship*, 88.
14. Brueggemann. *Psalms and the Life of Faith*, 129.

Bibliography

Alter, Robert. *The Art of Biblical Poetry*. New York: Basic Books, 2011.
Braun, Gabriele G. *God's Praise and God's Presence: A Biblical-theological Study*. Eugene, OR: Wipf & Stock, 2020.
Bonhoeffer, Dietrich. *The Cost of Discipleship*. London: Hassell Street, 2021.
Brueggemann, Walter. *From Whom No Secrets are Hid: Introducing the Psalms*. Louisville, KY: Westminster John Knox, 2014.
———. *The Prophetic Imagination*. Minneapolis: Augsburg Fortress, 2001.
———. *The Psalms and the Life of Faith*. Edited by and P. D. Miller. Minneapolis: Augsburg Fortress, 1995.
Chace, Sharon R. *Biblical Poems Embedded in Biblical Narratives*. Eugene, OR: Wipf and Stock, 2020.
Ellington, Scott A. *Risking Truth: Reshaping the World through Prayers of Lament*. Eugene, OR: Pickwick, 2008.
Gorman, Michael J. *Participating in Christ: Explorations in Paul's Theology and Spirituality*. Grand Rapids, MI: Baker Academic, 2019.
Hopkins, Denise Dombkowski. *Journey through the Psalms*. Rev. and exp. ed. Danvers, MA: Chalice, 2002.
James, Elaine T. *An Invitation to Biblical Poetry*. Oxford: Oxford University Press, 2022.
Peterson, Eugene H. *As Kingfishers Catch Fire: A Conversation on the Ways of God Formed by the Words of God*. New York: Hodder & Stoughton, 2017.
Strawn, Brent. "The Psalms and the Practices of Disclosure." Foreword to *From Whom No Secrets are Hid: Introducing the Psalms,* by Walter Brueggemann, xiii–xxiv. Louisville, KY: Westminster John Knox, 2014.
Streett, R. Alan. *Songs of Resistance: Challenging Caesar and Empire*. Eugene, OR: Cascade, 2022.
Waltke, Bruce K., James M. Houston, & Erika Moore. *The Psalms as Christian Worship: A Historical Commentary*. Grand Rapids, MI: William B. Eerdmans, 2010.

www.ingramcontent.com/pod-product-compliance
Lightning Source LLC
Chambersburg PA
CBHW062006220426
43662CB00010B/1249